Quarterly Essay

CONTENTS

Quarterly Essay is published four times a year by Black Inc., an imprint of Schwartz Publishing Pty Ltd
Publisher: Morry Schwartz

ISBN 186 395 1415

Subscriptions (4 issues): $49.95 a year within Australia incl. GST (Institutional subs. $59.95). Outside Australia $79.95. Payment may be made by Mastercard, Visa or Bankcard, or by cheque made out to Schwartz Publishing. Payment includes postage and handling.

To subscribe, fill out and post the subscription form on the last page of this essay, or subscribe online at:

www.quarterlyessay.com

Correspondence and subscriptions should be addressed to the Editor at:
Black Inc.
Level 5, 289 Flinders Lane
Melbourne VIC 3000 Australia
Phone: 61 3 9654 2000
Fax: 61 3 9654 2290
Email: quarterlyessay@blackincbooks.com
http://www.quarterlyessay.com

Editor: Chris Feik
Management: Sophy Williams
Editorial Co-ordinator: Caitlin Yates
Publicity: Meredith Kelly
Design: Guy Mirabella
Printer: Griffin Press

FOREWORD

In an earlier *Quarterly Essay* I analysed the campaign of the politicians and their supporters who were determined to repudiate the conclusions and deny the cultural meaning of the Human Rights Commission report into Aboriginal child removal, *Bringing them home*. More recently many of the same people have lent their support to the task of sending home the recent wave of asylum seekers who fled to Australia from the tyrannies of Iraq, Afghanistan and Iran. This coincidence provided the title for this essay.

There have been a number of excellent books on Australia and the "fourth wave" of asylum seekers, in particular Peter Mares' *Borderline*, David Marr and Marian Wilkinson's *Dark Victory* and Frank Brennan's *Tampering with Asylum*. None, however, focus on the impact of politics, policy and law on the asylum seekers themselves. Their experience is at the centre of this essay. Some of the issues in it are approached from a different angle than in earlier work. Some – like the Pacific Solution and repatriation – have never been dealt with at length before. The purpose of the essay is to allow readers to understand better what these asylum seekers and refugees have already endured and to help convince as many Australian citizens as possible that both the continued detention of asylum seekers and the planned program of repatriation of refugees are wrong. The recent announcement by Mark Latham, that the Australian Labor Party intends to show "compassion" for refugees, gives reason for hope.

In the deepest sense this essay is a work of collaboration. Between 1999 and 2003, I supervised David Corlett's doctoral thesis on asylum seeker policy in Australia. During this time we became friends. More recently we have begun to work together on a research project concerning the repatriation of asylum seekers and refugees. David Corlett carried out much of the primary research on which this essay is based. He has spoken extensively with many asylum seekers still inside the detention centres and with many refugees on temporary protection visas. He has corresponded and conducted phone conversations with asylum seekers and refugees and with their families in places as far afield as Iraq, Afghanistan and Nauru.

I have relied upon David Corlett's own writings on asylum seeker policy at many points and on his drafts for different parts of this essay. I have also been influenced by the conversations we have had over the years. Without David's resourcefulness, enthusiasm and intelligence this essay could never have been written. Nevertheless for its final form and its contents and tone I am solely responsible.

The research for this essay was made possible through a grant from the Myer Foundation. We are grateful to the Foundation and its CEO, Charles Lane. The research was also supported by the Edmund Rice Centre, the Refugee Council of Australia, Amnesty International Australia, the Christian World Service of the National Council of Churches in Australia, Uniya/Jesuit Refugee Service, the Catholic Commission for Justice, Development and Peace, the Asylum Seeker Project of the Hotham Mission and the Victorian Foundation for Survivors of Torture. The essay, however, does not in any way claim to represent their differing views.

Thanks are also due to Elaine and Geoff Smith for their generous support; to Morry Schwartz, Chris Feik and Caitlin Yates; to Father Tony Pearson, Jackie Everitt, Marion Le, Ngareta Rossell, Francis Milne, Keysar Trad, Pearl Longden, David Manne and to the many other people who have forwarded information and facilitated contact with individual asylum seekers and refugees.

Scores of refugees and asylum seekers have trusted David Corlett with their stories. Some are retold in this essay. It is never easy to speak of the terrible experience of dislocation and, as has often been the case, abuse. Both David and I hope that we have done justice to these people.

Robert Manne, March 2004

This essay is part of ongoing work. Anyone who would like to make contact should email d.corlett@latrobe.edu.au.

| SENDING | Refugees and the New Politics |
| THEM HOME | of Indifference |

Robert Manne with David Corlett

THE ROAD TO NAURU

> At a rough guess the years 1914–22 generated between four and five
> million refugees. This first flood of human jetsam was as nothing to
> that which followed the Second World War, or to the inhumanity
> with which they were treated.
>
> —Eric Hobsbawm, *Age of Extremes*

Between 1976 and 1981 some two thousand Vietnamese arrived on
Australia's northern shore. Despite considerable popular hostility and
media stories about armadas, criminal gangs and the introduction of
exotic disease, the Fraser government accepted all these people as
refugees. For the government to have rejected those fleeing from a regime
against which Australia had recently fought would have been regarded
by many anti-communist Coalition supporters as a great betrayal. As the

Prime Minister, Malcolm Fraser, understood, to have rejected them so shortly after the abandonment of the White Australia policy would also have undermined the belief that Australia had truly changed. Fraser was both an anti-communist and an anti-racist.

To its credit the Labor opposition, under both Gough Whitlam and Bill Hayden, acted with political decency. No issue would have been easier to exploit than this. The Vietnamese boat people were accepted as refugees, not on the basis of individual assessments but, on the recommendation of the United Nations High Commission for Refugees (UNHCR), as a collective group. There was at this time in our history no thought of mandatory detention. Indeed, if the Vietnamese had been locked up there would have been a conservative revolt. The refugees were housed in comfortable hostels and provided with generous social welfare and settlement assistance and English-language classes. All were offered permanent residence in Australia. All eventually had the right to apply to have close family join them here.

To stem the arrival of boats, the Fraser government became actively involved in the international diplomacy which aimed to find a solution to the Indochinese refugee exodus. As part of its involvement, the government promised Malaysia and Indonesia that it would take a generous quota of refugees from their holding camps. From the political point of view the planned admission of ten thousand Indochinese refugees each year was far less sensitive than the spontaneous arrival of a considerably smaller number in boats. During the 1980s, 177,000 Vietnamese were invited to Australia as refugees or as part of the country's official migration program. Due in part to the government's policies, no asylum seeker boat arrived between 1981 and 1987.

The road that led to Nauru began, then, not in 1976 but in November 1989 when a boat carrying twenty-three asylum seekers from Cambodia arrived at Pender Bay in Western Australia. In March and June 1990 two further asylum seeker boats from Cambodia arrived. All the asylum seekers on these boats were immediately placed in administrative detention

pending a decision on whether or not, according to Australia's interpretation of its obligations under the United Nations Convention on
Refugees, they were to be offered protection.

There were three main reasons why this "second wave" of boat people
– which continued until 1994 and which included, among the seven
hundred or so who arrived, the Cambodians as well as some Vietnamese
and Chinese nationals – was treated far more harshly than the first wave
had been. The Cold War was now over. Virtually no one in Australia felt
special sympathy for these people, on what one might call ideological
grounds. Furthermore, at the time of their arrival the Australian Foreign
Minister, Gareth Evans, was deeply involved in the complex diplomacy
surrounding the Cambodian Peace Plan, one sensitive item of which was
the repatriation of the Cambodian refugees in the Thai border camps.
To admit that conditions inside Cambodia might still be capable of pro-
ducing bona fide refugees would be politically embarrassing. It was far
easier to characterise the Cambodians as illegal immigrants or, as Prime
Minister Bob Hawke famously called them on one occasion, "queue
jumpers", who had journeyed to Australia not because of political persecution but simply to achieve a better economic life.

The third reason for their harsh treatment arose from the questionable
legality of detention at this time. In 1985 the High Court had decided
that the question of refugee determination was not exclusively a matter
for decision by government but could be reviewed by the courts. Between
1989 and 1991 the Cambodians were shunted around the country and,
in 1991, placed inside Australia's first special-purpose asylum seeker
detention centre at Port Hedland in the remote north-west. One reason
for this was to make it more difficult for lawyers to contact them.

In May 1992 the detention of asylum seekers was found, in the Federal
Court, to be unlawful. Section 88 of the *Migration Act*, which had provided
the basis for the Cambodians' detention, allowed merely for the short-
term detention of stowaways. In anticipation of this judgement, legislation
was rushed through the parliament restricting damages to falsely detained

asylum seekers to $1 a day. Much more importantly this interim legislation provided a secure statutory basis for the detention of all asylum seekers who arrived in Australia without a valid visa. The detention would last until the asylum seeker had been granted a visa or removed from Australia. Such detention was to be unreviewable by the courts.

The new legislation was soon put to the test. In December 1992 the High Court found mandatory detention lawful, with the proviso that its purpose was not to punish or to deter; it was to be used solely as an instrument of migration control. At much the same time the Hawke government introduced new legislation which balanced unreviewable mandatory detention with a Refugee Review Tribunal. The Tribunal offered asylum seekers whose claim for refugee protection had been refused the possibility of an independent "merits review". An asylum seeker unsatisfied with his or her RRT decision could appeal to the Federal or on rare occasions the High Court. Such an appeal, however, would be concerned exclusively with whether or not the Tribunal had decided the case according to law. The Federal Court could order a new Tribunal hearing, but it could not make a judgement on the substance of the case. If unsatisfied with the RRT decision, the asylum seeker could make a final appeal to the Minister's discretion, a discretion which was, in lawyer's jargon, both "non-compellable" and "non-reviewable". As Philip Ruddock would later put it, the asylum seeker's "safety net" was the Minister for Immigration. By 1992–93 the basic foundations of the contemporary Australian asylum seeker system had been laid.

Between 1994 and 1997 a "third wave" of boat people arrived in Australia seeking asylum. Some were so-called Sino-Vietnamese, ethnically Chinese refugees who had fled Vietnam and been resettled in southern China under a UNHCR-brokered scheme, the Comprehensive Plan of Action. Others were Vietnamese refugees from the Galang Refugee Camp in Indonesia. Still others were Chinese nationals. Initially, in 1994, some of these third-wave asylum seekers were accepted by Australia on refugee or humanitarian grounds. However, after the *Migration Act* was amended in late 1994, and repatriation agreements concluded with the Chinese government, virtually all the Sino-Vietnamese, the ex-Galang Vietnamese and the Chinese nationals were successfully, if brutally, removed. Some Vietnamese were forced into an aircraft bound hand and foot. There were violent protests at Port Hedland. Nevertheless, from the point of view of the Hawke and Howard governments, during the period of the third wave the system of detaining, assessing and, where possible, removing unauthorised boat arrivals "worked". Figures tell the story best. Between 1995 and 1998 fifty-four boats arrived spontaneously, bringing with them 1434 people. Of these 170 were accepted as refugees; eighteen (East Timorese) were granted bridging visas; 1246 were despatched. When the Howard government took office in 1996, Philip Ruddock discovered two hundred or so Chinese boat people still in detention. He thought even this number too great.

During 1999 the flow of Chinese and Sino-Vietnamese boat people dried up. The message had finally got through. Those who reached Australian shores would be sent home. On the other hand, in 1999 more boat people arrived than during the entire period of the second and third waves. Most of these asylum seekers came from Iraq and Afghanistan. Of the handful of Iraqis and Afghans who had reached Australia between 1996 and 1998, all had already been accepted as bona fide refugees. It was almost certain that the new arrivals would be as well. For the Australian asylum seeker system a kind of crisis had arrived. It is with Australia's treatment of these people that this essay is concerned.

Why had these people come to Australia in search of protection? By 1999 there were 2.5 million Afghan and 600,000 Iraqi refugees, according to the figures of the United Nations High Commission for Refugees. In the same year more than 20,000 Afghans and 30,000 Iraqis applied for asylum in the Western world. In the following years numbers grew. By the late 1990s the political conditions for the refugees from Iraq and Afghanistan, who had sought sanctuary in contiguous countries – Iran, Pakistan, Syria – had begun to deteriorate. Those who were poor had no alternative but to stay put. Those with even meagre resources or property to sell began, in increasing numbers, to turn to people smugglers offering passages to countries of possible safety in the West, where lives could be rebuilt. According to the accounts of many of the Iraqis, Afghans and, later, Iranians, one of the cheapest passages at the time was to Australia. By 1999 a route had been opened up, involving, essentially, flights from one or other country in the Middle East to Malaysia (where visas for Muslims were unnecessary); movement by sea or air from Malaysia to Indonesia; sea passage on an often barely seaworthy fishing boat from Indonesia to one of Australia's Indian Ocean territories, Christmas Island or Ashmore Reef.

The passage from the Middle East to Australia via Indonesia became common only in the second half of 1999, at the time of Australia's involvement in the politics of East Timorese independence. Although it cannot be proved, it seems likely that at this time the Indonesian authorities turned a blind eye to the activities of the people smugglers as a way of registering their displeasure at Australia's meddling in East Timor.

The arrival of the asylum seekers from Iraq, Afghanistan and, soon after, from the Islamic theocratic state of Iran as well, raised serious problems for the Australian government and people. In assessing their response, the following seem to us the most pertinent facts. According to Australia's historical experience, the number of "unauthorised" asylum seekers who arrived by boat between 1999 and 2001 – around 9500 in total – was large. According, however, to the recent experiences of North America and especially Western Europe, which by the late 1990s received several hundred thousand asylum seekers each year, the number was small. The first three waves of boat people came from the Asian region. Although those who now arrived had no historical or geographical relationship to Australia, their claims to refugee status were as powerful and plausible as any claims could be. After the 1970s the region from which they had fled had experienced a kind of perpetual turmoil – the Iranian Islamic revolution; the consolidation of Baathist totalitarian rule in Iraq;

the devastating eight-year Iran–Iraq war; and in Afghanistan, worst of all, the Soviet invasion, the resistance of the mujahideen, the rise of the fearsome fundamentalist Islamic Taliban regime. In its ferocity, this turmoil was almost equivalent to the "age of catastrophe" that had overtaken Europe between 1914 and 1945. By the late 1990s the political conditions in Iraq and Afghanistan and, less dramatically perhaps, in Iran, were comparable to the conditions which had created the Jewish refugee crisis in Central Europe in 1938–39 or the post-war flight of millions from the imposition of Stalinist regimes throughout Eastern Europe. No one ought to pretend that the unanticipated arrival of the Iraqis, Afghans and Iranians did not pose real legal, administrative, political and ethical problems for Australia. However these problems arose not because these people were not genuine refugees. They arose, rather, precisely because the overwhelming majority of them were.

With the arrival of these asylum seekers the Australian government had no alternative – unless it were to renounce its signature to the UN Refugee Convention – but to assess the validity of their claims for protection. Until those claims had been assessed it was, of course, predetermined that all would be administratively detained until a visa was granted or the failed asylum seeker removed from Australia. The government was, however, clearly alarmed. Two initiatives were taken. As early as June 1999, very heavy fines and long jail sentences were legislated for those responsible for organising the passages of the asylum seekers to Australia. Even more importantly, a new form of temporary protection visa for all "unauthorised arrivals" was introduced by regulation in October 1999. Asylum seekers found to be refugees were now to be granted three years' temporary protection.

When the Vietnamese boats arrived in 1976, the Fraser government and the anti-communist intelligentsia understood and strongly sympathised with their flight from Hanoi's rule. When, however, the Iraqi and Afghan boat people began arriving on Christmas Island and Ashmore Reef in the spring of 1999, they had no significant political friends in

Australia and were greeted by the Australian government with an undisguised hostility. On the road to Nauru this was an important moment.

In 2003 the Prime Minister spoke to the Australian people with real eloquence about the shocking brutality of the regime of Saddam Hussein, in preparation for the US-led invasion. Yet not once between 1999 and 2001 did he or any minister in his government explain to the Australian people the kind of terrifying conditions from which the asylum seekers from Iraq, Afghanistan or Iran had fled. Prior to September 11 the Australian people knew next to nothing about these regimes. In the absence of such understanding, the Minister for Immigration, Philip Ruddock, was able to conduct a very successful campaign of scaremongering and disinformation.

Ruddock's first significant move was to claim in November 1999 that Australian intelligence revealed ten thousand people from the Middle East, including entire villages, were uprooting themselves and setting out for Australia. To speak of whole villages suggested economic not political motivation. To speak of the Middle East, rather than Iraq or Afghanistan, inhibited even rudimentary political understanding. To speak of the imminent arrival of ten thousand excited the oldest Australian nightmare, of alien invasion from the north.

For those who had already arrived, Ruddock's characterisation was different. On 22 September 1999 he informed the parliament that he had been deeply disturbed by reports that the "very generosity of our refugee determination system" had attracted these unwanted people. On arrival, the new asylum seekers had demanded "Pert 2-in-1 shampoo" or to see "orthodontists" at once, "something", he pointed out, "many Australians would like to be able to do free of charge".

The most recent asylum seekers were not only insolent, they were also wealthy. Ruddock divided asylum seekers into two clear types – the worthy and unworthy – which resembled the nineteenth-century distinction between the respectable and unrespectable poor. Worthy refugees waited patiently in a Third World camp. Unworthy refugees used their money to engage the services of people smugglers. Willingness to pay people smugglers stripped unworthy refugees of any claim to sympathy. It represented, in them, a kind of indelible moral taint. In a speech on the asylum seeker problem delivered to a meeting of the Anglican church synod in Sydney in July 2001, Ruddock argued thus:

> I could characterise the task for both of us in familiar terms of doing good and fighting evil.
>
> The good is extending our compassion and welcome to refugees who have no other option.
>
> The fight against evil is against the exploitation by people smugglers of people desirous of a better life and the resultant abuse and the distortion of the system that has been set up to support refugees.

Ruddock had by now convinced himself that his struggle to keep asylum seekers from Iraq, Afghanistan and Iran from reaching Australia was part of a fight of good against evil. He regarded the money spent on processing asylum seeker claims in Australia and the West, as opposed to the money spent on the worthy refugees in the camps, as utterly "obscene".

Although the number of refugees around the world exceeded fourteen million at this time, from which Australia took an annual quota of four thousand (with eight thousand additional humanitarian places), Ruddock consistently described those who reached Australia as "queue jumpers". For the situations these people really faced, a refugee lottery or, even better, a refugee heap was a more appropriate metaphor than a refugee queue.

Nor were these people, according to Ruddock, only jumping queues. They were also "stealing places" from the worthy refugees Australia wished to help. How so? In 1996, for its own reasons, the Howard government had decided to link the onshore and offshore dimensions of Australia's humanitarian migration program (onshore applicants comprising arrivals in Australia by sea or air). As a consequence of this decision, the greater the number of "onshore" places given to refugees the fewer the number of "offshore" humanitarian places Australia would allot. This linkage was not written in the heavens; it was a Howard government choice. Apart from the empty moralising from a position of comfort involved in the idea of "stealing places", did Ruddock really imagine that those who fled to Australia via the Indonesian route had the kind of detailed knowledge of Australia's migration regulations which 99 per cent of Australians did not possess?

Not only were the asylum seekers queue jumpers who stole the places of worthy refugees, they were also, according to Philip Ruddock, "forum shoppers" who on their journey to Australia had passed through a number of countries in which they had been "safe and secure". These countries included Iran, Pakistan, Syria, Jordan, Malaysia and Indonesia. Anyone who was willing to listen to asylum seeker accounts of the perils of existence in countries such as these understood the utter unreality of Ruddock's concept of "safe and secure". It might have been inconvenient for Australia that the asylum seekers from Iraq, Afghanistan and Iran had the audacity to hope to rebuild shattered lives in a country where the rule of law and respect for human rights was strong. But it was hardly a moral failing or an instance of selfishness on their part, as Ruddock's use of the idea of "forum shopper" was meant to suggest.

Nor was it just for Ruddock to describe the asylum seekers as "illegal migrants" or as "illegals". Australia was one of the first signatories to the United Nations Convention on Refugees. The central purpose of the Convention was to create a world where those who fled from persecution in their homelands could move in search of sanctuary under the ultimate protection of international law. It was reasonable to speak of the people who reached Australian territory as "asylum seekers" and as "unauthorised arrivals" before their refugee claims had been assessed. But to describe them routinely as "illegal immigrants", or simply as "illegals", both defied the spirit of the UN Convention and encouraged popular misunderstanding and hostility – as was, no doubt, the government's intent.

Between July 1999 and June 2000 a little over four thousand asylum seekers, predominantly from Iraq, Afghanistan and Iran, reached Christmas Island or Ashmore Reef. It is unlikely that the asylum seekers had even heard about mandatory detention and temporary protection visas or that the impoverished Indonesian fishermen the people smugglers paid to bring them knew about the lengthy prison sentences they risked. What was certain, however, was that Australia's deterrent measures were not working. In the Middle East the Minister for Immigration sought the co-operation of governments in preventing the movement of asylum seekers. In Indonesia he offered Australian money to finance an island detention camp, an offer which Jakarta, with fresh memories of the international criticism it had received over its Vietnamese refugee camp at Galang, repeatedly refused. As an alternative the Australian Federal Police were sent to co-operate with Indonesian counterparts in anti-people smuggling operations, as was Australia's external spy agency, ASIS, in August 2001. To general amusement, the Department of Immigration even produced in June 2000 a video for distribution in the Middle East showing Australia as a land of desert, crocodiles, snakes and sharks. Despite all these initiatives nothing seemed to work. Between July 2000 and June 2001 an almost identical number of asylum seekers arrived via the Indonesian route as had come in the previous year.

More than eight thousand asylum seekers had now arrived in the space of two years and the existing detention centre system was unable to cope. The Curtin airbase near Derby in the far north-west had to be recommissioned. In the South Australian desert, at Woomera, a new centre was hastily built. In these centres, particularly in the remote or desert camps, conditions were especially harsh. On one famous occasion Ruddock boasted that they were not designed to be "holiday camps". The detention centres became sites of disorder and despair, of riots, arson, mass escapes, self-inflicted wounds, sewn lips, hunger strikes, suicide attempts.

On the grounds that the privacy of asylum seekers needed to be protected, journalists were not permitted to conduct interviews inside the detention centres. Film was, however, taken outside them at times of major disturbance, which created for the Australian public an enduring image of the asylum seekers as wild, irrational, hysterical, dangerous and manipulative. Even more importantly, whenever a disturbance occurred the Minister was available to offer his interpretation of what this kind of behaviour meant. Sometimes he suggested that asylum seekers' actions stemmed from their cultures. Sewing lips together, he remarked on one occasion, was a practice repugnant to Australians. Sometimes he suggested that the asylum seekers were trying to take advantage of the natural kindness of Australians, by what he routinely described as their "inappropriate behaviours" and occasionally as their "antics". One thing, however, was clear. The asylum seekers would never achieve "the outcomes" they desired by "moral blackmail" of this kind. Ruddock had no intention of conducting any negotiations under conditions of what he called "duress". Through the combination of the television images of savage asylum seekers and the Minister's invariably pitiless interpretation of their cries for help, a terrible coldness settled on very many Australians' hearts. This failure of sympathy was a crucial way-station on the road to Nauru.

In the first three weeks of August 2001 six boats arrived with more than 1200 asylum seekers on board. Evidence about government intentions at this time is difficult to interpret. On 8 August, at a meeting of the National Security Committee of the Cabinet, the Chief of the Defence Forces, Admiral Chris Barrie, was asked to investigate what action the Navy might take to create what was called a "thick grey line" across the Indian Ocean. This suggested a policy of military deterrence was already under consideration. On 23 August the Minister for Immigration announced plans for two major new detention centres at Singleton in New South Wales and Port Augusta, South Australia in addition to those at Darwin and Brisbane, which had previously been announced. This suggested that the government anticipated large numbers of asylum seekers would continue to arrive. What was the Prime Minister's view? On 17 August, following the arrival of a boat-load of 345 asylum seekers, he was challenged, on

Melbourne radio, about the failure of his policy. What, he replied, are we to do? "We are a humanitarian country. We don't turn people back into the sea ..." If the Prime Minister was already thinking seriously about military measures, it is unlikely that he had come to a firm decision by that time.

On 26 August, in response to an alert from Australia, the Norwegian cargo vessel MV *Tampa* rescued 433, mainly Afghan, asylum seekers en route to Australia. The Prime Minister now made up his mind. With his decision Australia changed. The *Tampa* sailed towards Christmas Island. Australia refused it permission to enter her territorial waters. Because of his fears about the health of the people he had rescued, the captain disobeyed. Australian troops boarded the *Tampa* and soon transferred its human cargo to a naval vessel, HMAS *Manoora*. An Australian legal action to bring the asylum seekers to Australia was mounted. By mid-September it had failed. Australian public opinion exploded in favour of the government's decision. The Labor opposition was badly scared.

Over the next fortnight or so the Australian asylum seeker system for dealing with boat arrivals was radicalised. Within Australia new legislation was passed with opposition support. To prevent the use of Christmas Island and Ashmore Reefs as the landing points for boats bringing asylum seekers to Australia, both were excised from the Australian migration zone. Penalties for people smuggling were increased. The courts were all but excluded from interference in government's handling of asylum seeker cases, a measure the High Court effectively rebuffed within eighteen months. The temporary visa system became even more harsh. The legal definition of a refugee was made far narrower than it had previously been.

While these laws were passing through the parliament, in the atmosphere of heightened tension over border security following the terrorist attacks of September 11, one of the most secretive and bizarre military actions in the history of the Australian defence forces, Operation Relex, was mounted in the Indian Ocean, against a flotilla of thirteen asylum seeker boats. One of these boats sank, with 353 drowned. Questions would later be asked about whether Australia had been in a position to mount a rescue operation. Some boats were sent back to Indonesia. Some were not able to be. As a result of the boarding of the *Tampa* and Operation Relex, 1500 asylum seekers fell under Australian military control.

What was to be their fate? New Zealand agreed to provide homes for up to 150 of the *Tampa* rescuees. Nauru and Papua New Guinea agreed to create "processing centres" on their soil. Since 1999 Australia's asylum seeker policy had followed an increasingly punitive logic. By September 2001 – to the general applause of a majority of Australians and to the dismay of a bewildered minority, now called the "elites" – Australia had arrived at a situation which would once have been thought inconceivable in what the Prime Minister had recently called a decent "humanitarian" country – the military repulsion of asylum seekers followed by their detention in offshore tropical detention centres until such time as their refugee status was determined. The Australian system for dealing with asylum seekers had finally reached its logical conclusion, at Nauru.

The system – based around mandatory detention, temporary protection and the Pacific Solution – was incomparably the harshest in the Western world. Only one task remained. It was to prepare to send the overwhelming majority of fourth-wave refugees and failed asylum seekers home.

> England has got to be true to herself. She is not being true to herself
> while the refugees who have sought our shores are being penned up
> in concentration camps ...
>
> —George Orwell, *The Lion and the Unicorn* (1941)

According to section 196 of the Australian *Migration Act*, all "unlawful
non-citizens" are to be detained until either removal or deportation or
until they are granted a visa allowing them to stay. To remove any doubts
from the minds of judges and lawyers, subsection (3) makes clear that
no one can be released from detention "even by a court". It was under
section 196 that all the 9500 or so fourth-wave asylum seekers were
detained.

To understand what happened to them under this section of the Act a
collective portrait is required. On arrival all asylum seekers were con-
veyed to a detention centre – the most important of these being the
remote and desert camps, Port Hedland (established in 1991), Curtin
(September 1999) and Woomera (November 1999). Many asylum seekers experienced, at first, a bewildering process known as "separation
detention", which might last for days or weeks or months. One purpose
of this was to "screen out" the few hopeless claims. Once this process was
complete the remainder, the overwhelming majority, waited in one of the
detention centres for an Immigration Department "primary decision" on
their protection case to be made. No one knew how long this process
might take. According to the figures released by the Department, in late
1999 eighty per cent of primary decisions were made within eight
months (by definition one-fifth took longer); by early 2001 the same
proportion were made within four months. Of the 8500 or so Iraqi or
Afghan applicants during the fourth wave, over 80 per cent were successful at the primary stage. The success rate of the Iranians was much
lower. Even after the asylum seekers had been accepted as bona fide

refugees they were not immediately released from detention. Character and security checks might take extra weeks or even months. Between 2000 and 2002 ASIO checked 5986 unauthorised arrivals and discovered not one threat.

Almost 90 per cent of the asylum seekers rejected at the primary stage lodged an appeal with the Refugee Review Tribunal. A high proportion of Iraqi and Afghan appeals were successful at this stage (in 2001–02, 87 per cent and 66 per cent respectively). These appeals would, however, require further months to be spent in detention. Almost half of those whose appeals to the Tribunal were unsuccessful went to the Federal Court. All the Federal Court could do was to return the case to the Tribunal if certain errors in law had been made. The Refugee Review Tribunal rarely reversed an original finding. Even more rarely the High Court heard an appeal. By the time the appeals process was exhausted many asylum seekers had spent two years or more in detention.

Only a small number of the fourth-wave asylum seekers whose claims ultimately failed were able to be removed, for complex reasons examined later in this essay. Very few agreed to return home voluntarily. Failed asylum seekers faced the prospect of a term of indefinite imprisonment. So determined was the Department to keep failed asylum seekers locked up that it even fought tenaciously (although unsuccessfully) a Federal Court decision ('al Masri') which ordered the release of some stateless or Palestinian asylum seekers who were willing to be removed but had no country to which they could go (or get to). Inside the detention centres in October 2003 were 278 people who had been locked up for between two and three years; 89 for between three and four years; nine for more than four years. Most but not all of these came by boat. In February 2004 there were still more than three hundred fourth-wave asylum seekers in detention. Of these the largest group were the Iranians.

Of the 9500 asylum seekers who had been in detention since 1999, for many months or for years, by 2003 ninety per cent or so had eventually been granted a temporary protection visa. Most had fled from the

Taliban or Saddam Hussein. Of these 9500, a little under two thousand were children, all of whom had spent months or years in detention.

During the fourth wave, the network of immigration detention centres constituted, in our opinion, the most inhumane and destructive quasi-penal institutions in Australia's post-federation history – where the inmates were treated more harshly than in the Japanese prisoner-of-war camps at Cowra, or the wartime internment camps at Hay and Tatura for German (often Jewish) and Italian aliens transported here from Britain during the early part of the Second World War, or even than in the worst of the inter-war Aboriginal internment settlements, like Queensland's Palm Island or Moore River in Western Australia.

In the period between late 1999 and early 2002, when there were sometimes up to three thousand asylum seekers in the overcrowded detention centres at any one time, social explosions were common – like the mass breakouts of mid-2000, or the serious riots and arson at Woomera or at Port Hedland in January 2001, where tear gas and water cannons were deployed, or the mass Woomera hunger strike, involving 259 people over sixteen days in January 2002. Throughout this period there were also countless incidents of self-harm in the detention centres, where inmates tried to hang themselves or slashed their wrists, or beat their heads repeatedly against internment walls, or threw their bodies on barbed wire, or sewed their lips together, or simply drank shampoo. In one eight-month period, between 1 March and 31 October 2001, the records of Australian Correctional Management (the private contractors paid to run the detention centres) show 264 official reports of incidents of self-harm. Almost certainly this figure was an underestimate. To the detention centre staff at this time such acts were commonplace. The clinical psychologist at Woomera told ABC television that when he arrived in March 2002 there were forty-eight people under observation thought to be at risk of suicide or self-harm. In May 2002 a member of the government's Immigration Detention Advisory Group, Paris Aristotle, explained, once more to ABC television, that the "culture of self-harm" and the levels of "depression and anxiety" within the Woomera detainees had become "endemic" and had "reached quite a staggering" level. (To the Department of Immigration this should have come as no surprise. It had itself advised the parliament in 1993 that among the long-term Cambodian detainees "depression and anxiety" had reached levels described as "acute".)

Why did the experience of mandatory detention prove so devastating for so many of the fourth-wave asylum seekers? On arrival many of those who fled from Iraq, Iran or Afghanistan – think, say, of the very many Hazaras who reached Australia and who had been a special target of Taliban ferocity – were already badly wounded people who had experienced in their own lives, and in the lives of their families, levels of political savagery and fear beyond the imagining of most native-born Australians. After fleeing their homelands many had lived precariously in countries of first asylum, such as Iran or Pakistan or Syria. Many had found their weeks in Indonesia less than "safe and secure". Some were badly shaken by the sea journey in an overcrowded, unseaworthy fishing boat.

Few of the asylum seekers anticipated or understood their isolation and detention in unmistakably prison-like conditions in a country they believed would offer hope and sanctuary. The philosopher Simone Weil once pointed out that there exists in every human being, despite all the evidence to the contrary, an almost inexpungeable expectation that they will be treated justly. Many asylum seekers were unbalanced by, and never really recovered from, the sense of injustice which overcame them following an imprisonment unconnected with the commission of any crime. Quickly the asylum seekers came to understand that their future would be determined by the outcome of a legal decision. They did not know, nor could they be told, how many months they might have to wait until the decision would be made. They had no way of properly understanding the logic of the legal process that would determine the outcome of their lives. They could not predict the likelihood of success or failure of their cases in a decision-making process notoriously arbitrary and inconsistent. In the quest for a visa, all were involved in a Kafkaesque

Trial. Adverse decisions seemed utterly random or, perhaps, grounded in racism. Those in the desert or remote camps, especially, had great difficulty in communicating adequately, or at all, with a lawyer.

While waiting on their decisions or the decisions on their appeals, the men who had come alone often could not contact their families. They eventually learned that, under the system of temporary protection, even if their cases were successful they could not hope soon to be reunited with those they had left behind. Many felt guilty for abandoning wives and children. Others felt ashamed about being imprisoned in Australia, a fact that they found difficult to explain and which their families found difficult to understand. Sometimes their claims to be imprisoned in Australia were simply disbelieved.

For those who came with family, detention presented problems of a different kind. With the incarceration, in single institutions, of men, women and children, dangers of sexual abuse of both wives and children were real. As parents disintegrated psychologically under the stress of detention, they knew they could not offer their children the kind of protection and care they now desperately required. Because of the terrible atmosphere that pervaded the detention centres – the fights between inmates and guards, the self-harming acts and attempted suicides, the general despair – parents understood that their children were witnessing scenes which might scar them for the remainder of their lives.

For all these reasons and many more – including the indifference or contempt or brutality of the guards and the utter boredom that filled each day – a kind of madness descended on those held in mandatory detention for months, and in particular on those who gradually came to realise that should their claim for protection ultimately fail they would be caught indefinitely between the hopelessness of life in detention and the overwhelming fear of what might happen to them if they were forced to return to the countries from which they had fled.

*

In early 2001 members of the federal parliamentary Joint Standing Committee on Foreign Affairs, Defence and Trade paid a visit to the Australian detention centres. They were shaken by what they stumbled upon. Some were "shocked by the harsh picture presented by the exterior of some of the centres: double gates, large spaces between high fences topped with barbed or razor wire". For others "the strongest memory ... was the despair and depression of the detainees, their inability to understand why they were being kept in detention in isolated places, in harsh physical conditions with nothing to do."

The delegation learned of people from Iraq and Afghanistan who had been in detention since June 1999. They were told that even when women were taken to doctors outside the centres they went in handcuffs. One detainee told the delegation of the six daily musters he experienced, one at 3 a.m. The delegation met an inmate who had been imprisoned for years and simply wanted to go home. "I prefer to go back and be killed." They were told by several inmates that prison was preferable to life in a detention centre. At the punishment area of Port Hedland, Juliet Block, they were appalled at the physical conditions, the showers which were not working, the toilets without seats. Here they met an inmate who told them that, while on hunger strike, he had been handcuffed violently and taken with his child from Villawood in Sydney to Port Hedland. Both were left locked up in an isolation cell in Juliet Block for thirteen days. A woman wept openly when speaking to the delegation about the effect of long-term detention on her children. At Villawood they met a medical practitioner, a long-term detainee, who outlined for them what he called "immigration detention syndrome". The symptoms were aggression and major character change. "In the end if left in a centre," he argued, "everyone will develop this syndrome." The delegation apparently agreed. One of its most important recommendations was that detention should be limited to a period of fourteen weeks.

As soon as the report was published, the Minister dismissed the report in general as "clearly superficial" and its fourteen-week recommendation as extraordinarily "naive". In 1992 the parliament had imposed a nine-month limitation on mandatory detention. In 1994 this legislative provision had lapsed. Over time sensibilities had coarsened. By 2001 the Minister's conscience was untroubled by the prospect of indefinite detention for people who had committed no crime. For some of the delegation, he scoffed, the visits to the detention centres had been the "most significant event of their lives". "Such people have not had the benefit of life's experience."

Nor, apparently, had the Human Rights Commissioner, Dr Sev Ozdowski, who visited every detention centre between February 2001 and January 2002. Ozdowski witnessed "persuasive desperation and depression" and "serious mental health difficulties" among the long-term detainees. He encountered one woman who had been kept in isolation detention for seven months; detainees who complained bitterly to him about being treated by their guards as criminals; detainees who felt their illnesses were not taken seriously. Ozdowski learned that it was "common practice" to refer to detainees by number rather than by name. He met an Afghan man whose hands were trembling, who told him that both his children had become "severely depressed". He personally encountered "several examples" of children who showed "signs of depression and mental illness". Ozdowski was told by detainees of the torture and the trauma they had experienced before reaching Australia. At Villawood, the resident psychologist informed him that between 20 per cent and 25 per cent of the inmates suffered from a very serious mental illness, post-traumatic stress disorder.

Dr Ozdowski's report had little public impact. The Department of Immigration was singularly unimpressed. In his preface the Human Rights Commissioner had made some general remarks about the current asylum seeker policy and the Australian tradition:

> It is wrong to suggest that the integrity of the border protection system is threatened by the small, sad flotilla of leaking boats with their desperately fragile cargo of asylum seekers. We can maintain a

system of visas and identity, security and health checks without stamping all over our 'fair go' heritage.

These remarks angered the Department Secretary, Bill Farmer. "I have concerns that the preface to the report is written in a manner that could be construed as inflammatory and biased in its analysis of the detention environment ... the purpose of the preface seems to be to attack the policy of mandatory detention." Obviously Farmer regarded such an attack as illegitimate. It is not clear what he considered the role of Australia's Commissioner of Human Rights to be.

At the time Ozdowski's report was published the Chairman of the United Nations Working Group on Arbitrary Detention, Louis Joinet, visited Australia. After his visit to the camps he wrote possibly the most devastating critique of the Australian system of mandatory detention.

Joinet did not believe the mandatory detention of asylum seekers necessarily breached international law. He did believe, however, that the way in which the policy was practised in Australia did. The deprivation of the liberty of an asylum seeker had to be, as he put it, "proportionate" to the reasonable policy ambition of the state. How could a system, he asked, which "results in the detention of children, elderly or sick people and others in a vulnerable situation" be said to be "necessary to achieve the aims of an immigration policy"? In addition, under international law anyone deprived of liberty was entitled to a hearing before an independent court. In Australia this possibility did not exist.

Like the previous visitors, Joinet was shocked by what he saw and heard – by the children who attempted suicide or by the Iranian family at Port Hedland (two sisters, three retarded children) whose situation was "tragic to behold". But he noticed certain legal oddities as well. Joinet was astonished that inmates were taxed $1000 if their cases before the Refugee Review Tribunal failed. "It is paradoxical", he noted with drollery, "that while in very many countries a tax is payable on visas issued, Australia requires payment for a refusal." He was even more astonished to discover that the inmates were presented with bills for tens of thousands of dollars for the cost of their detention. With his own eyes he had seen a bill for $214,346. When he asked to see a contract between the Australian government and the private corporations that ran the detention centres (and even punished the inmates), his request was refused on the grounds that it was a "business secret". All this seemed to Joinet – both as judge and human rights defender – genuinely strange.

Australian officials explained to him that the purpose of the policy of mandatory detention was to deter asylum seekers. He did not realise this to be an admission of a breach in the law, according to the unambiguous High Court ruling of 1992. Officials also explained to him that the policy was extremely popular. Perhaps so. But would they continue to support this policy, he inquired in his report, if they were aware that at least according to "the knowledge of the delegation" – the foremost authority in the field – "a system combining mandatory, automatic, indiscriminate and indefinite detention without real access to court challenge is not practised by any other country in the world"?

While in Australia investigating the detention centres Joinet had used the phrase "collective depression syndrome", for which he was officially reproached. During the period of the fourth wave of asylum seekers many attempts were made to investigate the truth of this description in a more systematic way.

One of the more important of these studies was, strangely enough, carried out by a long-term detainee, an Iraqi physician, Dr Aamer Sultan, in collaboration with a former Visiting Clinical Psychologist at Villawood, Kevin O'Sullivan. From a questionnaire answered by most long-term detainees at Villawood, he discovered that of the 33 people surveyed, 32 experienced chronic nightmares, 31 chronic feelings of helplessness, 28 chronic depressive symptoms, 23 suicidal ideation, 19 required psychotropic medication, 18 displayed psychomotor retardation, 13 had paranoid delusions and 7 full-blown psychosis.

Another important, although methodologically curious, study was

undertaken by a team of psychologists led by the major student of the subject of the mental health of the asylum seeker detainees, Dr Zachary Steel.
Steel sought to assess the impact of long-term detention among a single
ethnic group (unnamed in the published results) in a single remote camp
(also unnamed). Because his team would never be given permission by the
authorities to conduct the research in the detention centre, it was conducted, not altogether satisfactorily, with the use of interpreters via the
telephone. Parents were asked, in one study, to answer questions about
their children. The researchers summarised the answers thus:

> The children particularly reported being distressed by witnessing
> the frequent acts of self-harm and suicide by other detainees. All
> of the children witnessed the same act of self-harm by an adult
> detainee who repeatedly mutilated himself with a razor in the main
> compound of the detention centre. Children also described having
> witnessed detainees who had slashed their wrists, jumped from
> buildings, resulting in broken legs, and detainees attempting to
> strangle themselves with electric cords. At times, children witnessed
> their parents' suicide attempts, or saw their parents hit with batons
> by officers. A number also witnessed their friends and siblings
> harming themselves.

Steel's team, in assessing the children, used a standard diagnostic
instrument. Of the twenty children surveyed, 95 per cent experienced
major depressive disorder; 55 per cent suicidal ideation; 50 per cent
post-traumatic stress disorder and separation anxiety disorder; 25 per
cent had committed acts of self-harm; 20 per cent regularly wet their
beds. Steel's team also studied the children's parents. One hundred per
cent suffered a major depressive disorder; 86 per cent post-traumatic
stress disorder; 93 per cent experienced suicidal thoughts; 36 per cent
had engaged in acts of self-harm. The average length of stay in incarceration of those studied was already 2.1 years.

*

How can we best reveal the atmosphere inside the immigration detention centres, the spirit in which the policy of mandatory detention was administered, and the morality of incarcerating children? We can think of no better way than to tell the story of Shayan Badraie.

The Badraie family came from Iran. The father, Mohammed, is a Kurd, an educated man (a computer technician) and the member of an old religious sect, Al Hagh, long regarded by Iranian Shia clerics as a dangerous anti-Muslim heresy. After being granted a divorce from his first wife, who, he explained with embarrassment at a hearing of the Refugee Review Tribunal, had "shown interest" in another man, Mohammed remarried a Shia Arab, Zahra, so his son should have a mother. He had been granted custody over Shayan. According to Mohammed, Zahra converted to his faith. The family fled Iran in part because of the discrimination he experienced throughout his life when his religion became known, in part because of his involvement in university protests in 1999 which had led to mass arrests, and in part because, according to Sharia law, it was an extremely serious offence, in contemporary Iran, to convert a Muslim woman to what was regarded as a heretical non-Muslim faith.

The Badraie family arrived in Australia on an Indonesian fishing boat in March 2000. According to Mohammed the voyage was easy, the ocean smooth. Shayan was fascinated by the flying fish. The family was taken straight to Woomera. At the time Shayan was a bright, inquisitive and sensitive five-year-old.

Within days of arriving and again in April and late July, Shayan witnessed riots, which were brought under control by guards with batons, water cannons and tear gas. Shayan began to experience panic attacks; he became withdrawn and lost his appetite. By July 2000 (all of this has been scrupulously investigated by the Human Rights Commission President, Professor Alice Tay) the Immigration Department had learned of Shayan's problems. Nothing was done.

In December 2000 Shayan saw a man holding a shard of glass to his chest, threatening to kill himself. Shayan began to wake up frequently at night holding his chest. He wanted to sleep only during the day. On 4 January 2001 Shayan saw another inmate threatening to kill himself by jumping from a tree. A nurse and counsellor at Woomera, Wayne Lynch, who was negotiating with the man, saw Shayan standing close by, watching. He tried to convince him to move away. Shayan soon observed a dispute between his father and an Australian Correctional Management guard who was mocking inmates with a masturbatory gesture. On 20 January, for reasons unknown, the entire Badraie family was transferred to the punishment block at Woomera, the Sierra Compound. Shayan had been told, and believed, that only bad people were sent to Sierra. He saw his father grappling with a guard, being forcibly restrained. He saw his mother, in protest, being abused by an ACM guard, told to "fuck off." Soon after, he witnessed another suicide attempt. By now Wayne Lynch, who was taking an interest in the family, was deeply alarmed. On 22 February 2001 Lynch sent a memorandum to the ACM manager, copied also to the Immigration Department. Shayan's state was described as "bed-wetting, nightmares, anorexia, insomnia, fearfulness". By this time Shayan had been formally diagnosed as suffering from post-traumatic stress disorder. Something had to be done. The Minister was entitled to release the family under section 417 of the Act. This was not considered. Rather, on 3 March 2001, the Badraies were transferred to another detention centre, Sydney's Villawood. Six days later they learned their appeal to the Refugee Review Tribunal had failed.

During March Shayan was taken to Westmead Hospital for observation. A consultant psychologist, Dr Timothy Hannan, reported that he was waking up ten times each night, screaming in terror. Hannan warned that if Shayan was returned to Villawood he was in danger of suffering "prolonged stress syndrome". Shayan was, nevertheless, returned.

On 30 April Shayan saw a Villawood inmate who had slashed his wrist and was bleeding profusely. He believed the man was dying. The scene became a recurring subject of his drawing. Three days later Shayan was returned to Westmead for rehydration. Three senior medical and psychological staff warned that if this "acutely traumatised" child were to be returned to Villawood all his symptoms would recur. Shayan was, nonetheless, returned. He was analysed by a psychologist at Villawood, Dr Ramesh Nair, who wrote about Shayan's fear of the fences, the barbed wire, the uniforms. Unless he was removed from Villawood there was every prospect of "long-lasting psychological damage". Shayan was sent back to hospital. He was now neither eating nor drinking. From Westmead, the Head of the Department of Psychological Medicine, Dr David Dosseter, wrote twice to the Minister pleading for his help. Shayan, he pointed out, could not return to Villawood. He needed his parents. He could not be kept permanently at Westmead Hospital. No help from the Minister was offered. Between May and July 2001 Shayan remained in Westmead, for want of any alternative, hospitalised.

Under the *Migration Act*, section 417, the Minister has the power to grant protection visas in cases of humanitarian concern. On 24 May an application on the Badraie family's behalf was made to the Minister for humane consideration. On 7 June the application was strongly supported by a Department of Immigration officer. His memorandum included lengthy extracts of the opinions of Hannan, Nair and Dosseter on the dire state of Shayan's mental health. The Minister rejected the application. In his wisdom he decided that Shayan would return to Villawood. On 9 July it was done. Shayan again stopped drinking and eating. Between 14 July and 9 August he had to be sent to Westmead Hospital, on nine separate occasions, for rehydration.

The Badraie family was by now supported by the lawyer Jackie Everitt and the author of the participant-observer psychological study at Villawood, the inmate Dr Aamer Sultan. Through their efforts, on 13 August *Four Corners* showed film of a limp and lifeless boy, who neither ate nor drank nor spoke, cradled in the arms of his father. The Minister now had a problem.

On 14 August Ruddock appeared on the 7.30 *Report*. He dropped a hint that there might be more to this case than met the eye. Kerry O'Brien insisted that he explain. "Well, I'll simply say that the child is not the natural child of the mother ... it's a stepchild." Four times he referred to Shayan as "it". Being a stepchild seemed to Ruddock as plausible an explanation of Shayan's catatonia as the fact that he had been imprisoned for eighteen months during which time he had witnessed his parents' private distress and public humiliation and three serious detention centre riots and four serious suicide attempts. Asked then and later why he had refused to release the Badraies from detention under section 417, the Minister had two responses. If he gave visas to the family, other truly worthy refugees would thereby be deprived. And if he gave them protection, was it not likely that other families would come forward with faked cases of mental illness in their child? He would not allow the system of mandatory detention to unwind. No exceptions could be made. The Minister was soon supported by two of the country's most influential right-wing columnists. In the Melbourne *Herald Sun* Andrew Bolt effectively accused Mohammed Badraie of deliberately starving his son. In the Sydney *Daily Telegraph* Piers Akerman accused him of belonging to the murderous Iranian Revolutionary Guard and, by quoting a newspaper article written by his first wife, of having kidnapped Shayan.

On 16 August an Immigration official visited the Badraies. There could be no question of releasing the family under section 417, or even – as the Act permitted – of removing them to a house or an apartment the Minister designated as a place of detention. The family were told they must return to Iran. Meanwhile Mohammed was asked to consent to the fostering out of his child, a course of action which the Department had been repeatedly warned against by the psychologists and medical practitioners who had become acquainted with Shayan. There are things the Howard government has done which are almost impossible to believe. This is one. How could a government Minister separate a dangerously ill six-year-old boy from his one source of support? How could the

Australian people tolerate behaviour of this kind from a Minister of the Crown?

With no real choice in the matter the family allowed Shayan to go to a foster home. His parents were permitted to visit him three times a week. Shayan, in foster care with an Iranian family, was "clingy", "angry", needed his foster parents by him when he went to sleep and when he woke, wet his bed, begged to be reunited with his family. After four months the foster family gave up. The Minister now agreed to grant bridging visas to Zahra and Shayan's baby sister, who had been born in detention. Mohammed remained locked up.

The story has an ironical ending. The Badraie case was referred back to the Refugee Review Tribunal by decision of the Full Federal Court. In August 2002, because of the persecution the family might face in Iran as a result of Zahra's conversion to Al Hagh, the Badraies were discovered to be refugees after all. We have it on good authority that the Minister was furious.

The Badraies took their case to HREOC, which found, on the basis of the treatment of Shayan outlined here, that their human rights had been seriously violated by the behaviour of this minister. HREOC suggested that the family were owed an apology from Mr Ruddock and $70,000 in compensation, suggestions which the Minister declined to accept. In October 2003 the Badraies commenced civil action against the Commonwealth in the New South Wales Supreme Court.

The Badraies were offered only temporary protection. It is not impossible that, in the future, if it is decided that their protection needs have ended, and if the Badraies are unwilling to be repatriated to Iran, they might find themselves in a detention centre once again. This is a prospect that terrifies Shayan, now eight years old. His father tries to tell him it will not happen. Shayan is unconvinced.

TEMPORARY PROTECTION

> Aloofness became the new attitude of the British services; it was a
> more dangerous form of governing than despotism and arbitrari-
> ness ...
>
> —Hannah Arendt on bureaucracy

Like the Badraies, virtually all fourth-wave asylum seekers were offered
only temporary protection if found to be genuine refugees. They moved,
accordingly, out of detention centres into what some called their "second
punishment" and others an "open prison".

It is not, strictly speaking, true, as some have claimed, that the introduction of the Temporary Protection Visa on 20 October 1999 was the
first time Australia had experimented with non-permanent asylum. In
June 1989, in the aftermath of Tiananmen Square, a tearful Bob Hawke
gave a personal pledge to the twenty thousand students from the People's
Republic of China currently in Australia that none would be forced to go
home. From the viewpoint of the public servants in the Department of
Immigration, this was probably the most irresponsible sentence ever
uttered by an Australian prime minister. Though almost none of the
Chinese students were genuine refugees, all were guaranteed asylum. The
permanent protection visa, in addition, guaranteed family reunion rights.
In 1991 the Department convinced the government to offer only temporary visas to avoid the possibility at least of family reunions. However,
as a visa type restricted to the Chinese students was, self-evidently, dis-
criminatory, temporary visas had to be extended to all onshore asylum
seekers. The experiment did not last. The prospect of trying to remove
more than 20,000 Chinese students against their will somehow did not
appeal. In 1994 the temporary visa scheme for onshore refugees was
quietly abandoned by Paul Keating.

This was not Australia's only experience with temporary protection
visas. In 1999, as NATO was preparing to go to war against Serbia,

hundreds of thousands of Kosovars began fleeing to neighbouring countries. With the help of vivid television images, a wave of sympathy for them swept the West. The ever-cautious Immigration Department did not want Australia involved in the offer of Kosovar sanctuary. The Prime Minister, John Howard, smelling political trouble if Australia appeared ungenerous, disagreed. On 5 April Philip Ruddock announced that Australia would not be offering refuge to Kosovars. On 6 April the Prime Minister made clear that we would. Four thousand soon arrived. The Department limited the political damage by means of carefully crafted legislation. The Kosovars were offered what were called "temporary safe haven visas". The Minister alone would determine how long the refugees might stay. They were not allowed, while in Australia, to apply for a permanent protection visa. Later in the year "temporary safe haven" visas were offered to 1450 East Timorese fleeing pro-Indonesian militias following the independence referendum. In both these cases Australia was offering asylum not to individuals with a well-founded fear of persecution but to a collective group whose lives were at immediate risk because of the breakdown of order in their homelands. The short-term safe haven offered to the Kosovars and the East Timorese in 1999 was the kind of temporary protection, becoming increasingly common in Western countries during the 1990s, of which the United Nations High Commission for Refugees thoroughly approved.

In 1998 Pauline Hanson's far-right One Nation Party suggested something considerably more radical – the granting of temporary visas for all twelve thousand onshore and offshore refugees and humanitarian places allocated by Australia each year. The political nation dismissed the idea with derision and contempt.

> What One Nation would be saying [Philip Ruddock argued, in a characteristic response] is that [refugees] have no place in Australia. They are only to be here temporarily … Can you imagine what temporary entry would mean for them? It would mean that people

would never know whether they were able to remain here. There would be uncertainty, particularly in terms of the attention given to learning English and in addressing the torture and trauma so they are healed from some of the tremendous physical and psychological wounds they have suffered ... I regard One Nation's approach as being highly unconscionable in a way that most thinking people would reject.

In 1999 some of the most traumatised, most physically and psychologically wounded refugees on earth, fleeing from Saddam Hussein and the Taliban, began arriving on Australian territory. Because these people had not waited patiently in camps or in the contiguous countries where their lives were either insecure or under threat, and had used whatever resources they had to buy a passage to freedom, what was utterly "unconscionable" to Ruddock in 1998, what was repugnant to all "thinking people", became in 1999 for both the Minister and most of the Australian people a matter of merest commonsense.

The decision to offer only temporary protection visas to all "unauthorised arrivals" was taken, with Labor Party support, as soon as significant numbers of Iraqi and Afghan asylum seekers began to arrive. The reasoning behind the decision was clear. These people were not welcome in Australia. Nevertheless it was obvious that most were genuine refugees. For political, legal and moral reasons repatriation to Iraq and Afghanistan was both impossible and unthinkable. No one yet dreamt of a military solution. Some new powerful and effective deterrent measure, in addition to harsh mandatory detention, was required. It had been noticed, as soon as the fourth wave of asylum seekers broke on Australian shores, that most were single men. It seemed likely that many hoped to bring their children and their wives after them. The two most important conditions attaching to the temporary protection visa were the prohibitions placed on family reunion applications and on the right to return to Australia if the visa holder subsequently travelled abroad. If Australia made it obvious that all possibility of reunion with close family had been ruled out in advance for "unauthorised arrivals", even if they were granted refugee status, the necessary message that Australia was a refugee-unfriendly country would, at least eventually, sink in.

In parliament the Minister was confident the idea would work:

> Why do I argue that the temporary entry arrangements are likely, over time, to have some impact? It is because most of the people who are arriving in Australia unlawfully by boat ... are essentially unaccompanied males. They are leaving behind spouses and children ... The fact is they have an expectation that their partners will be sponsored under the Refugee and Humanitarian Program.

Conditions attached to the temporary protection visa would disappoint that expectation. The asylum seekers would look elsewhere. Or so it was hoped.

In addition to the motive of deterrence, there was, in the conditions applying to the temporary protection visa, a deliberate policy of punishing, or at least not rewarding, those who arrived without invitation in Australia. The TPVs were released from detention, transported to a city centre and provided with some basic advice; after this the Immigration Department took little further responsibility for what happened to them. Those who helped them noticed that panic often set in on the second night after their release. Under the conditions of their visa they were granted bare subsistence welfare – Medicare and the Special Benefit – but denied those things which offshore refugees were known to require – most importantly in the short-term, accommodation assistance, and in the long-term, the 510 hours of English language tuition of which the Minister had spoken in attacking the One Nation refugee policy in 1998.

Self-consciously, in short, the Commonwealth government created a two-class refugee system. It discouraged State governments from offering the temporary visa holders assistance. It warned voluntary agencies it subsidised not to use Commonwealth funds on TPVs. Usually unemployed, living commonly in overcrowded rooms so barely furnished that even social workers used to poverty were shocked, the TPVs existed, as was planned, on the very outer margins of Australian society.

Mandatory detention and temporary protection visas succeeded in making the lives of the asylum seekers even more unpleasant than they might otherwise have been. In their deterrent function, however, they almost altogether failed. In 2000–01 as many asylum seekers reached Australia as in 1999–2000. If anything the anti-family reunion conditions of the temporary protection visa acted not as a deterrent but as a perverse incentive. Rather than discouraging single males, they seem if anything to have encouraged the departure for Australia of whole families and of wives and children with husbands or fathers already here. As Mary Crock and Ben Saul have noticed: "In 1999 children made up only 13 per cent of asylum seekers arriving by boat. After the introduction of the temporary protection visa, (by) 2001 the proportion of children on boats rose to 30 per cent." For the public servants in Canberra temporary protection visas were a blunt instrument of policy. For refugees they were both a source of further suffering and yet another impediment to be overcome in the rebuilding of their lives, as the next story reveals.

In 1998 Ahmed Alzalimi, a member of the Iraqi middle class and a university graduate in history, became, because of his political connections, a target of the Baathist secret police. For two years Ahmed remained hidden in a house outside Baghdad. In 1991, during the post-Gulf War chaos, he fled to Iran. Some time after, Ahmed returned briefly to the Kurdish region of northern Iraq to marry Sondos Ismael, a young Iraqi woman from a family connected to the Alzalimis. Her father had been executed by Saddam Hussein; her uncle had "disappeared". Shortly after their marriage, Ahmed took Sondos to Tehran. They had four children, a son who died shortly after birth and three daughters. Throughout the 1990s the couple lived a hand-to-mouth existence in Iran in an increasingly politically precarious world. They received some financial assistance from Ahmed's brother in America. By the late 1990s, at a time of heightened official Iranian propaganda directed at Iraqi exiles, their greatest fear was of forcible repatriation to Baghdad and inevitable execution. In 1999 Ahmed decided to seek asylum in Australia with the help of people smugglers. Despite his obviously forged papers, Iranian authorities were only too happy to assist him to leave. At this time Ahmed believed he would be able to arrange for his wife and daughters to travel to Australia after him lawfully. He was precisely the kind of asylum seeker against whom the conditions of the temporary protection visa had been designed.

Ahmed Alzilimi arrived on Australian territory in late 1999, having taken the familiar Malaysia–Indonesia route. He became one of the early detainees at Curtin. The conditions of his reception in Australia were not, to put it mildly, what he had anticipated. He felt humiliated by them and violated. He was especially shocked to discover that he could not even apply to have his wife and daughters join him. For the first five months he and his fellow detainees had no contact with the outside world. After eight months he was released on a temporary protection visa. He was transported to Brisbane and travelled to Sydney.

In Tehran, Sondos Ismael learned of many fatherless families in a situation similar to hers who had managed to make their way to Australia. She paid a people smuggler US$5000 to take her family to Australia. She arrived, with her sister and her daughters, in Indonesia in October 2001. In reality by this time – with Christmas Island and Ashmore Reef excised from the Australian migration zone and Operation Relex in action – Sondos had no chance of reaching Australia. Nevertheless, the Egyptian people smuggler Abu Quessai arranged for Sondos and her family to board a grossly overloaded boat, which would eventually become known in Australia as SIEV-X. On 19 October, in international waters, SIEV-X broke up very rapidly and sank. 353 died; 44 survived. Sondos was one of the survivors. She tried to hold onto her daughters but failed; they disappeared into the ocean. Later Sondos was rescued by an Indonesian fishing boat. She realised now her sister had also drowned.

News of the sinking of the SIEV-X and the drowning of Sondos and Ahmed's three daughters reached Australia at the mid-point of the 2001 federal election campaign, a campaign dominated by the overwhelming popularity of the Howard government's military solution to the asylum seeker problem. This was an issue which the government exploited brilliantly and ruthlessly and which the opposition – with the smell of a possible electoral catastrophe in its nostrils – greatly feared.

Can a political nation lose touch with moral reality? What happened next convinces us that it can. Ahmed Alzalimi was an Iraqi refugee living in a flat in Sydney, so devastated by the news of the death of his three beloved daughters that he had ceased to eat and drink. Sondos Ismael, his wife, who had seen her daughters drown, was now in a guesthouse on the outskirts of Jakarta, in the grip of a grief inexpressibly profound. In Australia a political question arose: should Ahmed be permitted to visit his wife? To the government the answer was clear. According to the conditions of the temporary protection visa, a refugee who travelled outside Australia had no right of return. Had not these conditions been designed precisely to prevent family reunions? The Prime Minister pointed to the dangerous precedent that might be established: If the government allowed Ahmed to visit Sondos, would not other TPVs soon come to it with similar requests? For his part, the Immigration Minister explained the situation like this: It was simply not true that Australia was preventing Ahmed from visiting his wife; it was merely unwilling to guarantee that he could come back. So frightened of the issue was the leader of the opposition, Kim Beazley, that he pointedly declined all invitations to criticise the government's unwillingness to allow Ahmed to go to his wife. At this moment in our history, the cardinal Orwellian political virtue of "common decency" was nowhere to be found.

If Ahmed could not go to Jakarta, surely it was at least possible that Sondos might be brought to Sydney soon? According to the legal process acceptable to the Department of Immigration, the refugee claims of all SIEV-X survivors were to be assessed by the United Nations High

Commission for Refugees. When the process was complete, all were discovered to be refugees. Australia agreed to take Sondos Ismael. In January 2002, three months after the sinking, Sondos was still in Jakarta. The Minister was unhappy about any suggestion of delay. On the contrary, a spokesman said, "a view was taken" that the case "should be processed urgently". But in March she was still there. According to the Department, Sondos needed a document from Iran which certified that she was not a criminal. Despite considerable efforts such a document was not able to be prised out of the Tehran police, as the Department ought on the basis of past experience to have been able to predict. It was within the discretion of the Minister to waive this requirement. As it turned out, the Minister had not been so inclined. Sondos was reunited with her husband five months after the drowning of her children. The Minister's spokesman described the delay as "not unreasonable". Due to the "tragic circumstances", if anything, the case had been "expedited".

At present the family is in a curious legal situation. Ahmed is in Australia on an extension visa, his three-year temporary protection visa having expired. The couple's new baby daughter is on a temporary protection visa with two years or more to run. Sondos is on a five-year temporary protection visa granted to refugees in "third countries" accepted by Australia. The family has been promised that it will be allowed to stay until the expiry of Sondos's visa. At that time their protection needs will be reassessed. If they face no well-founded fear of persecution, the family can then be sent home to Iraq. Perhaps by that time Sondos will have found new strength. At present she is a broken woman, who each evening, Ahmed told us, makes beds for the three daughters she has lost.

In the atmosphere of border protection panic which followed the concocted *Tampa* crisis, the Minister for Immigration seized the opportunity to attach even more refugee-unfriendly conditions to the temporary protection visa. Before the September 2001 amendments, TPVs had to prove their continued need for protection after three years. If unsuccessful they were to be sent home. If successful they would become permanent residents. The amendments altered this. From now on even those TPVs who could prove they still needed Australia's protection but who had stayed for seven days continuously in a so-called "third country", and who could have sought and obtained "effective protection" there, would not be given a permanent home, only another temporary protection visa. In three years the process would be repeated. For refugees caught by this new regulation, permanent temporariness or eventual repatriation would be their lot.

The system had another twist. All those who had applied for a second protection visa before 27 September 2001 would be granted permanent residence (if their application was successful). Almost all those who had not yet applied would never be given permanency. The new law was not technically retrospective. It had, however, a profoundly significant retrospective impact on the lives of the 4400 unlucky TPVs who had not lodged their second-round applications by the deadline of 26 September. This new regulation was introduced without warning or amnesty. Did Canberra really need to remind these refugees once more that life was little more than a lottery?

It was not merely or even mainly the new regulations, however, that would determine the life chances of the TPVs. During 2002 and 2003 it gradually became clear that the future prospects of perhaps 9000 refugees would be determined by the unanticipated post-September 11 political situation in Central Asia and the Middle East. In 2001–02 a US-led coalition overthrew the Taliban and in March–May 2003 the regime of Saddam Hussein. Ninety per cent of the fourth-wave refugees had fled from Afghanistan and Iraq. Even though the post-invasion conditions in both countries were catastrophically insecure and growing worse, was it not likely that, in the changed political circumstances, most second-round protection applications of people whose first applications had centred on Taliban or Baathist persecution would fail?

This certainly was Canberra's hope. In December 2002 the Department sent letters to Afghan TPVs offering them a so-called "reintegration package" ($2000 per individual; $10,000 per family) in return for going home. In 1999 the temporary protection visa system was introduced primarily as an anti-asylum seeker deterrent. By 2002 it provided Canberra with the opportunity to try to send thousands of unwanted refugees home.

For the fourth-wave refugees this prospect has become the great nightmare of their lives. In 2002 and 2003 a number of studies were conducted into the lives of the TPVs. All were interested primarily in social service provision for refugees. All soon discovered that for the TPVs the overwhelmingly most serious issue was not inadequate welfare entitlement but the permanent threat of repatriation to the countries from which they had fled. One study, by Greg Marston in Victoria, put the point like this. "All research participants" considered matters like welfare benefits, employment and education opportunities, English-language tuition and so on as "second-order issues compared with the ongoing and deep uncertainty associated with the temporary protection".

The mental state of the TPVs was expressed most vividly by Paula Fernandes, the team leader of an Early Intervention Torture and Trauma Program which supported them:

> Most TPV holders present as anxious and agitated, full of unexpressed anger against the perceived injustice related to their detention experiences and the temporary visa status … They report headaches, gastro-intestinal disturbances and bodily aches and pains. Through denial, dissociation and thought suppression they have learned to alter an unbearable reality. The majority are bitter and feel forsaken by both "man and God" … As a result of prolonged repeated trauma, many TPV holders experience an intense numbing feeling of pain which they find difficult to articulate and express. Many describe this as "Burning in the Fire, but still continuing to Live".

So far as we are aware only one systematic study has been undertaken into the psychic impact of temporary protection and the fear of repatriation on these fourth-wave refugees, again by Zachary Steel and his team. The study was conducted among seventy-six TPV holders and thirty-seven refugee and migrant permanent residents from a single ethnic group. Participants were asked about their state of mind during the past seven days. Fifty-eight per cent of the TPVs and 28 per cent of the permanent residents reported having "terrifying thoughts" about the future; 64 per cent of the TPVs and 11 per cent of permanent residents reported "recurrent vivid images" concerning such events; 46 per cent of the TPVs and 5 per cent of the permanent residents had nightmares about the future; 57 per cent of the TPVs and 11 per cent of the permanent residents had experienced "sudden physical reactions" like accelerated heartbeat or shaking hands.

For refugees one kind of trauma therapy involves revisiting and thereby eventually neutralising the nightmare memories from the past. For the TPVs this is not possible. As the study puts it: "Standard treatments such as imagined exposure or testimony therapy appear to have a core assumption of safety." With the TPVs it is, precisely, future safety which cannot be assumed. For the psychic state discovered among these temporary protection visa holders a new term was invented – "anticipatory traumatic stress". The TPVs are the only group of refugees whose nightmares concern the future and not the past.

The fear of repatriation is experienced with great intensity by the Shia Hazaras of Afghanistan who fled from the vicious Sunni Taliban assault upon them in the late 1990s. One of these Hazaras was an educated man, Habibullah Wahedy, who became known among fellow Hazara refugees in Australia, because of his wisdom and his kindness, as Dr Habib.

Dr Habib arrived in Australia in October 1999 and spent his first seven months at Port Hedland detention centre. He had left behind him in Afghanistan a father and mother and a wife and three children, all of whom he dearly loved. According to his father, when he left Afghanistan he was "sound in body and in mind". Nonetheless he was badly scared by the Taliban, from whom he had escaped after a short imprisonment. Habib explained to the Department of Immigration officer who interviewed him that if he was threatened with repatriation he would kill himself. The Department delegate explained that in Australia threats of this kind would do him no good.

Habib was released from Port Hedland to Perth. After some time he moved to Murray Bridge in South Australia to a job as a boner at a meatworks, where the reliability of the Hazaras was already well known. Dr Habib became a respected leader in the small Murray Bridge Hazara community. Like many others, because he feared night thoughts and could not sleep, he took an evening shift. During the day he helped his fellow Hazaras as an interpreter.

Gradually Dr Habib began to disintegrate. He withdrew from a large shared house. He began to give away his possessions. He became, as did so many Hazaras, seriously depressed. Habib also became increasingly suspicious, believing that he was under constant surveillance; that his mail was being opened; that he was regarded as a terrorist; that, on account of his unusual command of English (a subject his father taught at university), his claims that he came from Afghanistan and that he had been persecuted there were now in doubt. In April 2003 his temporary protection visa was due to expire. Some of those who knew him believed that the "reintegration package" letter he received in December 2002, which many Hazaras interpreted as government-inspired psychological warfare to drive them away, had a particularly devastating impact on Dr Habib.

In early 2003 the South Australian Hazaras were shaken by two incidents. Two Hazara teenagers were killed in a car accident on the way from Melbourne to Adelaide. At much the same time news arrived of three Hazara refugees who were shot and killed while returning to Afghanistan from Pakistan.

On the evening of 2 February 2003 Dr Habib seemed in a normal frame of mind to the man with whom he shared a flat. He was not. Later that night Habib whispered into a tape recorder a rambling suicide note:

> I have no alternative but to kill myself … I am being followed … Unfortunately [my neighbours] may think I am a terrorist … I have $14,000 in my account … Also one year's worth of superannuation … Please take care of it so that my body is sent to Kabul … From the day I entered school … I was a bit simple and people took advantage … Father and mother forgive me. My children forgive me. Wife, I love you … I have to kill myself … I live in this land for 3 and a half years … I was thirsting to see my children, also my father and mother and sister and brother … But I realise I can no longer take these pains … I was being followed … My soul was being tortured … All the workers at T & R have been instigated against me … You can contact the Red Cross to take my body. Advise them to bury me in Karte Sakhi beside my grandfather. May God protect and help you. Goodbye.

Dr Habib then left his house, took off his shoes, climbed a telegraph pole and electrocuted himself. His body remained suspended on the tangled wires for twelve hours. Among the Murray Bridge Hazaras Dr Habib's death was deeply unsettling. Some said that they well understood why he had done what he had done. Some worried that they might be unable to resist the temptation to follow his example.

In Canberra the suicide of Dr Habib became, very briefly, a political issue. "There is a campaign here by some", the Minister argued, "to try to link his death to issues relating to his status. But I think if there are people who believe they know what his state of mind was, what was influencing him, then I think they bear some culpability." "I always lament when people who are in touch with individuals … don't get appropriate support and counselling." The government could hardly be expected, during the period of their waiting, to take each and every TPV by the hand.

THE PACIFIC SOLUTION

> Thou hast committed
> Fornication: but that was in another country,
> And besides, the wench is dead.
> —Christopher Marlowe, as quoted by T. S. Eliot

By late August 2001 it was obvious that the Howard government's asylum seeker deterrent measures – mandatory detention; temporary protection; tough anti-people smuggling penalties in Australia and disruption activities in Indonesia – had failed. The rescue of 433 mainly Afghan asylum seekers on 26 August by the MV *Tampa* could not have been predicted. The government's response to that rescue involved frantic behind-the-scenes improvisation. Nevertheless it is also true that by this time the creation of a new hard-line asylum seeker policy was a near-inevitability. The detention centres were overflowing. More asylum seekers had arrived by boat in August than in any previous month in Australian history. Intelligence reports suggested that considerable numbers of Afghans and Iraqis had already reached Indonesia. Public opinion, as measured in polls and focus groups, was overwhelmingly, indeed violently, opposed to allowing the boats to land. A general election was shortly due.

In the course of constructing this new policy, after 26 August, the first practical problem the government faced was what to do with the asylum seekers transferred from the *Tampa* to the *Manoora* and, thus, placed under Australian military control. Indonesia would not have them back. New Zealand was willing to take up to 150 women and children but no more. The UN Secretary-General refused to allow East Timor to become Australia's asylum seeker dumping ground.

Happily, the President of Nauru agreed to precisely this. By 12 September a formal agreement between the governments of Australia and Nauru had been reached. It was clear, nonetheless, that Nauru's capacity was limited, and unclear how many asylum seekers might try to reach

Australia in the coming weeks and months. Formal or informal soundings were taken in several Pacific countries – Kiribati, Tuvalu, Palau, Fiji, New Caledonia, Papua New Guinea. Of these soundings only one achieved success. On 8 October, thirty minutes before the formal beginning of the Australian election campaign, when the caretaker conventions of the constitution kick in and policy innovation becomes more difficult, an agreement between Canberra and Port Moresby was reached. By now Australia's bold new asylum seeker policy – the processing in offshore tropical-island camps of boat people Australia had been able to repel by military means but unable to force back to Indonesia – had emerged. It was christened by some wit in Canberra the Pacific Solution.

On the mined-out superphosphate moonscape of Nauru, two detention camps with plastic, wood and corrugated-iron barrack-style accommodation – Topside and State House – were hastily constructed by local labour and Australian military personnel. On PNG's Manus Island an old naval patrol-boat base, with views of both the sea and the jungle, was turned into a detention centre by surrounding it with wire and using the Nissan huts and converted shipping containers already there.

According to the constitutions of both Nauru and Papua New Guinea (but not Australia) detention of people who have committed no crime is unlawful. For this reason, Canberra suggested a legal fiction. Asylum seekers were admitted to both countries on a special visa, whose condition was the willingness of the visitors to wait permanently in "processing centres". If the visitors escaped, they were deemed to have breached the conditions of their visas and could be punished for the offence. They had, however, not been detained.

This was not the only curious legal dimension of the Pacific Solution. In regard to the creation and the administration of the detention camps, both Nauru and Papua New Guinea were willing to behave like client states. The Australian government wanted to ban all unapproved visits to Nauru and Manus Island – by journalists, lawyers, doctors, heads of NGOs, ministers of religion, concerned citizens and other troublemakers.

Australia always denied that it was responsible for these bans. It claimed the responsibility lay with the visa-granting countries, Nauru and Papua New Guinea, which everyone knew to be a lie. As a result of the ban, since the beginning of the Pacific Solution, near-complete secrecy concerning the condition of the detainees has been maintained by the government, accepted without serious dissent by the Labor opposition and tolerated by the Australian media without great fuss.

In return for its services to Australia, Nauru, which could not afford to pay its public servants or for much else, was offered $26.5 million – which included $9 million to pay for fuel; $4.7 million for its power and a desalination water plant; and $1 million for the Australian hospital bills owed by members of the island's elite. Papua New Guinea did not receive direct bribes. Instead, it seems, infrastructure improvements were made on Manus Island and, more importantly, it received its much-needed Australian foreign aid moneys in advance.

The contract to run the camps was given to the International Organisation of Migration (IOM), a non-profit company financed by Western countries to carry out some of their more complicated and morally distasteful international migration, asylum seeker and refugee tasks. IOM, however, did not run the camps alone. Inside the wire the security contract was awarded to a private company, Chubb. Outside the wire the government's Australian Protective Service kept guard alongside native army or police personnel. Food was supplied by a company called Eurest.

Following the *Tampa* crisis, until November 2001, thirteen Indonesian fishing boats with asylum seekers on board tried and failed to reach Australia. One, as we have seen, sank, killing 353. Four boats, with some six hundred on board, were intercepted by the Australian Navy and successfully forced back to Indonesia. Of the remaining eight boats, all of which were intercepted, some were unseaworthy, some were scuttled by asylum seekers, one simply sank while being towed. From those rescued by the *Tampa* and these eight boats, 1155 asylum seekers were transported to Nauru and 356 to Manus Island. Manus was predominantly an Iraqi camp, with small numbers of others mainly from the Middle East. Nauru was ethnically mixed, although here Afghans were sent to the larger Topside camp, on an abandoned football field, and Iraqis to State House. On Nauru the asylum seekers were sorted into three clear groups for bureaucratic purposes – *Tampa*, *Tobruk* and Christmas Island – according to the time and the mode of their arrival. On this basis each asylum seeker was allotted a coded number, by which they knew themselves and became, more generally, known.

At the beginning of the Pacific Solution, the United Nations High Commission for Refugees (UNHCR) agreed, with considerable misgivings, to an Australian request to process the *Tampa* group and those Iraqi asylum seekers taken to Nauru on the same boat, the *Manoora*. It refused to process subsequent Nauru transports or the Manus Island group. As a consequence, the Department of Immigration conducted all post-*Manoora* processings, adopting for the purpose the UNHCR system which the Minister admired, having always believed Australia to be a "soft touch" so far as refugee determination was concerned. According to this system, Pacific Solution asylum seekers were given an initial determination, without the benefit of legal advice. Those who were rejected had only one right of appeal, to a more senior UNHCR or Immigration Department official. After a second refusal the asylum seekers were expected, voluntarily, to return home. The processing philosophies of UNHCR and the Department of Immigration differed only in one detail. UNHCR believed wives and children of men already accepted as refugees should also be accepted. The Department disagreed. A number of women and children on Nauru and Manus Island, with husbands and fathers in Australia on temporary protection visas, were among the Department's rejectees. Eventually a solution to this problem was found. To Australia's shame, New Zealand allowed several such families to be reunited on its soil.

By the end of 2002 both UNHCR and the Department of Immigration had almost completed their asylum seeker processing. Approximately half the Pacific Solution asylum claims had succeeded while half had failed. Because the processing occurred before the invasion of Iraq, the success rate of the Iraqis was much higher than that of the Afghans, who had fled their homeland before, but been processed after, the fall of the Taliban. Among those who were found to be refugees only two countries offered to take significant numbers – New Zealand and Australia. Those who were accepted by New Zealand were granted permanent protection. Those who were accepted by Australia entered the purgatory of temporary protection: five years for those who had been rescued or intercepted before reaching an excised offshore place; three years for those who had set foot on Christmas Island or Ashmore Reef. Very occasionally Pacific Solution inmates were allowed to travel to Australia for medical treatment. An amendment to the *Migration Act* prevented such people from applying for protection while there. By 2003 the main problem for Australia was to convince the 800 or so failed asylum seekers on Nauru and on Manus Island (before the removal in July 2003 of its rump population to Nauru) to go home.

Because of the ban on all non-approved travel to Nauru, accurate information on the condition of the residents of Topside and State House is difficult to find. The only communication with outsiders the inmates have been allowed are letters, faxes, email and almost impossibly expensive telephone calls. A few remarkable Australians were so distressed when they learned about the situation of the abandoned detainees on Nauru that they came to dedicate their lives to befriending them and keeping constantly in touch. One of these Australians is Elaine Smith, a pharmacist from a coastal town in New South Wales. She allowed us to read the letters and the emails she has received from asylum seekers from the Topside camp in Nauru. To understand what has happened to them this correspondence is an indispensable source. From it a picture of the daily life of the Nauruan detainees can be drawn.

Nauru is extraordinarily hot and humid, a climate for which the

Afghans at least were unprepared. After some time the Topside barracks had airconditioners; the Iraqis in State House had to rely on the natural flow of air and fans. Nauru does not have enough fresh water. Very many letters complain about the perpetual shortages of fresh water for drinking and the brackish water for showering or washing clothes. "We are provided with … salty water for six hours a day," a Topside resident explained in May 2003. "We are provided with clean water too but just two hours a day running in eight taps." Many believed the desalinated water was affecting their kidneys. Some write about using rain water for fresh showers or even collecting drinking water when it rains.

There are many reports about the dreadful stench coming from the toilets at Topside and the problem of the mosquitoes that breed there. In early 2003, when there was an outbreak of dengue fever – a mosquito-borne disease – no one was greatly surprised. The food on Nauru is a reasonably frequent cause of complaint. Correspondents write of the blandness of boiled food, the use of old meat, more recently the absence of fruit and even bread. From time to time the letters report an outbreak of diarrhoea. One correspondent writes about being "poisoned" by camp food.

The International Organisation of Migration seems to do its best to entertain the adults and educate the children. There are satellite televisions for news and video recorders for showing films. Every once in a while inmates are taken on shopping expeditions or are taught by the local Nauruans to swim, a novel experience for asylum seekers from landlocked Afghanistan. Children attend local Nauruan schools. Some attend computer classes at camp in the afternoon. Many detainees are learning English. Among them, in September 2002, a soccer tournament was organised, with seventeen teams, two Arab and fifteen Afghan. "One of the most exciting matches", according to an Afghan competitor, "was the semi-final between 'Alamdar' and 'Iraqi' football teams. The people were very interested watching this match." Many detainees are still trying to live normal lives. One of Elaine Smith's correspondents is an artist.

"For portrait drawing I need a sculpture (a head of a man) to draw and teach. Can you please send me a cheap one?"

The tedium of daily life is occasionally interrupted by significant events. News of suicide attempts passes speedily through the camps. In December 2003 an Afghan carpenter tried to hang himself. He was cut down by a Chubb guard, handcuffed, sedated and taken to the Nauru police station. In Nauru attempted suicide is a crime. Four months earlier an even more significant event occurred at Topside, when a young man in apparent good health, a recent rejectee, suddenly cried out loudly from his bed at 5.30 a.m. and died instantly. A political struggle then broke out between the inmates and IOM over whether his body would be returned to Afghanistan or buried in Nauru. On this occasion, with the financial assistance of the young man's sister in Melbourne, the inmates had their way and the body was sent home.

Visits from prominent persons are also significant events. When members of the Afghan Embassy in Canberra came to Nauru in June 2003, Topside camp's astute political analyst noticed how, on the first day, they were sympathetic to the asylum seekers but on the second toed the Howard–Ruddock line. Almost all the detainees were impressed and encouraged when Senator Andrew Bartlett visited in June 2003, although he told them he could promise nothing. One detainee reported that when a woman in the Bartlett party heard of their plight she wept. For the detainees, however, a more memorable visit was that of the Minister for Immigration in February 2002. On this occasion Ruddock delivered a short, peremptory speech. People who tried to enter Australia illegally, "through a window", the Minister explained, would simply not succeed. The image of the window remained in the detainees' minds. According to the Topside political analyst, Ruddock was greeted by the camp's many children, whom he conspicuously ignored. The children returned to their rooms "with flowers in their hands". For "what was observed in their faces, I don't have suitable words".

Of course the visits that were most memorable of all were those of the assessors from UNHCR and the Department of Immigration. They were the source of endless speculation, rumour and complaint. These visits would determine the future shape of the detainees' lives.

Many of the inmates were already, on arrival at Nauru, in a terrible state of health. One young *Tampa* man, a supporter of women's rights against Islamic fundamentalists, had lost an eye and a leg after an explosion in Afghanistan. He had great trouble with his artificial leg. After returning from Melbourne with a new, ill-fitting one his stump began to bleed. His armpits became infected from the crutches and the sweat. His friends became disturbed because he would not leave his room. Others were concerned about an Iraqi woman who arrived from Manus Island with an extremely serious back problem, crippled by pain. She was one of those on board the boat where the asylum seekers were falsely accused by the Howard government of throwing their children overboard. Her back injuries occurred when she was winched out of the water by the crew of HMAS *Adelaide* after the boat had sunk. The Department of Immigration and IOM are trying to convince her and her husband, who has acute diabetes, to return to Iraq. Another of the correspondents describes his strange physical condition like this: the left side of his face burns as if he is being "destroyed by fire". He was referred to a psychiatrist.

Mental illness is, in the correspondence, the most common complaint. According to one correspondent, "All of the people look crazy"; according to another, "I have been suffering psychological problems since I have result of my last interview." And according to a third, "Believe me I am not remaining the same boy ... I used to be. Here I have lost my confidence, courage and tolerance. Sometimes I think why God create me in this world. Sometimes I think why I should not commit suicide ... I am 22 years old and already I am a useless man ... I am so sorry to make your heart sad but what should I do, these are the voice of my heart."

One of the correspondents is a nine-year-old Hazara boy. His mother's hand is broken; she is always crying. "My mother is too sad." The boy's father has lost his mind. He takes seven pills a day, cannot sleep, wanders about the camp at night, grows angry on occasion and, although normally loving, beats his children. The boy is certain that if his family is forced to go back to Afghanistan his father will be killed. "Please take us out of this prison." If you succeed, he promises, "my mother will be your servant."

Another writes: "The condition of the camp is as usual ... Really we are in Hell." Hell is by far the most common metaphor used by the detainees to describe the experience of Nauru.

In July 2002 Dr Maarten Dormaar of the Netherlands was appointed by IOM as psychiatrist to the residents of Topside and State House. Following his departure from Nauru in November 2002, Dormaar allowed three of his monthly reports to his employer to become publicly available. They represent the most important eyewitness accounts, from any Westerner, about the conditions of the inmates in the Nauruan camps.

In August Dormaar wrote as an empirical psychologist. He informed IOM that he had conducted a scientific survey of 118 Afghan adult males with problems of mental health. Dormaar divided these patients according to their age and the time of their arrival (*Tampa, Tobruk*, Christmas Island). He discovered that the older the asylum seeker and the longer they had been on Nauru, the greater was the likelihood that they would suffer mental problems.

> We conclude that the duration of distress is the major factor responsible in the difference reported in mental health cases. Apparently, there is a certain period of about three months that healthy young men like the group of asylum seekers in fact is or was, can sustain a rather normal level of functioning without clear symptoms of suffering or distress.

Dormaar's first report was sober but not without some hope that he could be of use. He informed his employer that he had planned a series of "stress management courses", mental health lectures, and even that he planned to interview "the quite scarce individuals that still seem to manage quite well". Perhaps they could become "role models" for others.

The tone of the September report was more sombre. Since last month there had been two main developments. A group of Iraqi rejectees had arrived from Manus Island. They had lost all hope, felt as if they were already dead and were indignant about Australia. "When I return to Iraq, Saddam will kill me quickly with a bullet. Here Australia is killing me slowly." The month had also been dominated by reactions to "final decisions", released from 6 September. To understand the deterioration of the asylum seekers' mental health, Dormaar argues, "social factors" must be analysed.

One is "despair". The decisions have gone badly, especially for the Afghans. They face a Sophie's choice between indefinite detention or returning to places they still fear. With regard to that choice they believe they receive "one-sided information"; that is to say, the Department lies to them about conditions inside Afghanistan to get them to go home. Even those accepted as refugees face "uncertainty". They do not know when they will leave for a new country or to which country they will go. If it is to Australia, they know that they will receive only temporary protection, which renders "futile" hopes of building a new life. All have become totally mistrustful of authority. Having been lied to constantly they have "lost all faith in fellow human beings". They have also lost all faith in the selection process. They have no access to legal advice. Their written statements are ignored. The Hazaras are certain that the Pashtun interpreters are racially biased. They are also "in limbo". IOM provides one five-minute satellite phone call home each month. Frequently the calls fail. In addition, "without access to the media the asylum seekers have no means to present their plight to the outside world".

Dormaar ended his September report with what he called a "clinical vignette".

A young man, 20 years of age, was seen for the first time. It took him close to an hour to tell his family history and background. He had lost all his brothers and sisters except one. Each time he had given details on one of them, he stopped and laid his head on the desk. Then, after a few minutes, he continued the interview.

By October Dormaar has become very angry. His anger is directed against the country which has treated the asylum seekers with such cruelty.

> The irony of incarcerating Muslims on an Island named after the birth of the Saviour bringing love and peace to mankind will escape Australia. It will also pretend to be oblivious to the violations of humane treatment and human rights (like having a fair trial), committed in its name to people whose only 'crime' has been that they have tried to 'get into the house via the window and Australia will not tolerate that'. (Minister Roddick [sic] in his speech to the asylum seekers during his visit to the camps …) …
>
> Effective banning of media in Nauru helps Australians to say, when all is over: 'we have not known of it.' Where else in recent history did people say so? Anyway, Australia is doing its dirty laundry in a small island that, for all practical purposes is its vassal state …
>
> Nauru cannot refuse the money and its big brother is aware of this … The 'processing centres' with their subjugated and desperate population under the tropical sun is like 'The Heart of Darkness'.

The references to Australian cultural crudity ("The irony … will escape Australia") and to the excuses of ordinary Germans under Nazism ("Where else in history did people say so?") and to Joseph Conrad's great anti-imperialist novel *Heart of Darkness*, all make one thing clear. This is the anger of a European directed at a country which he believes has utterly betrayed the values of a common civilisation.

On 15 November 2002 Maarten Dormaar resigned. He explained his resignation, in a speech to the staff, by telling a story about an early nineteenth-century Viennese doctor, Semmelweiss. Through observation and intuition, Semmelweiss came to grasp the connection between the appalling levels of disease within hospitals and the lack of basic hygiene. He tried to convince his superiors of the connection. He failed and was eventually forced from his post.

The practice of psychiatry on Nauru, Dormaar continued, was as futile as the practice of medicine in the filthy hospitals of early nineteenth-century Vienna.

> Mental health in its broad sense tries to promote physical and mental *well-being*. That is more than the absence of disease ... 1200, now some 850, mostly young men, women and children are kept in a prison-like situation for no other offence than to get a more safe and fruitful life than they could have in their own country ... They are constantly punished from day to day ...
>
> Mental health under these circumstances is like trying to use antibiotics in a pre-Semmelweiss hospital; the bare essentials of mental hygiene, like respect for a person's autonomy and integrity, are violated by those in power ...
>
> So now you know one of my main reasons to quit ... No self-respecting psychiatrist will accept to work under these deten-tion-like conditions.

When Dormaar's report became known in Australia, the Minister for Immigration was approached. Ruddock told his interviewer that he was not surprised to hear that the asylum seekers on Nauru were depressed. After all, they had failed to achieve the migration outcome they desired.

When Dr Dormaar resigned in November 2002, there were 850 asylum seekers on Nauru. By December 2003 only 284 remained. The majority of these were Afghan Hazaras. They viewed the situation in which they now found themselves in the following way.

Almost all seem to have believed that the determination process which had decided their fate had been, as they had informed Dormaar, utterly corrupted by the Pashtun interpreters both UNHCR and the Department of Immigration had employed. One put it like this. In Afghanistan Pashtuns killed Hazaras with "weapons"; on Nauru they were killing them with the use of the "pen". The Nauru Hazaras were extremely well-informed about the deteriorating security situation in their homeland. They knew, for example, that UNHCR itself had recently evacuated Ghazni province, from which many of them had fled, after one of its employees had been shot. They were also aware that one of the Nauru Hazara rejectees who had agreed to return to Afghanistan had recently been murdered. "Our life is in danger same as M. Muse Nazary," one wrote. They believed that most of the four hundred or so who had returned to Afghanistan had already fled. Of the thirty who left some weeks ago, one wrote to Elaine Smith on 12 August 2003, "some of them are in Iran and some … in Pakistan." From time to time messages arrived warning them not to go home. The Topside political analyst had left Nauru in late August 2003. In late September he sent the following message from Afghanistan to Nauru.

> My fellow Refugees … The danger of a new conflict, the existence of al-Qaeda and the Taliban … endanger the peace process of Afghanistan … They use heavy weapons and have killed thousands of people this year … I have not been able to find any peaceful place for living since I arrived in Kabul … Hundreds of returnees have left again … Afghanistan is still burning.

The asylum seekers almost all claim in their correspondence to have been told repeatedly by Immigration Department and IOM officials that their cases would never be re-opened, that if they did not agree to leave voluntarily they would in time be forcibly returned or, alternatively, abandoned to the whims of the Nauruan population who many, by now, had come to fear. "We had a meeting yesterday", one wrote in early December 2003, "with the IOM and DIMIA [the Department of Immigration], in which they told us they were going to finish with the Nauru mission and hand us to the Nauruan community ... They told us we had only one option which is to return to our country of origin." What, they often ask in their correspondence, are they to do? "If our homeland was safe and at peace we wouldn't stay here one second to waste our life." But if they return to Afghanistan they are certain their lives will be at risk.

On 10 December 2003, a hunger strike began on Nauru. The strike at first involved nine men, four of whom had sewn their lips together – a cultural practice learned from Port Hedland or Woomera and not Afghanistan. The slogan of the strikers was "Freedom or Death". In their manifesto they pleaded with the Australian people: "Do not forget us in your happiness". The strike spread rapidly. By 15 December it involved twenty-five men; by Christmas Day, forty-five.

All but one of the hunger strikers were Hazara men. Their spokesman expressed their world view and their despair with great lucidity and eloquence:

> We Hazara people were persecuted everytime and everywhere in different ways. I don't know what the crime we have committed is ...
> We escaped from Afghanistan to seek refuge in Australia but the Australian government rejected us and said you have not proved that you are refugees ... The Afghan government says you are not Afghan. When we migrate to Pakistan and Iran they say "Bloody fool Afghans! Why have you come?" They say that you have destroyed your country and now you are going to destroy ours ... There is not a place on earth for us to shelter. And as we are not capable of going to other Planets then where should we go?

For the first week the Australian government ignored the hunger strike. Nothing was more natural, in its dealings with asylum seekers, than the impulse to ignore such acts of desperation, which were now routinely interpreted as low-grade moral blackmail. When the silence was finally broken, the new Minister for Immigration, Senator Amanda Vanstone, claimed, astonishingly enough, that the strike had nothing to do with Australia. The word she used to characterise the protest was "unattractive". She had no pity for the strikers. Her sympathy was reserved exclusively for the hospital staff who had to treat and then treat again these impossible people. Her spokesman surprised a British journalist with his no-nonsense brutality. There was, he said, a simple solution to the strike. The Afghans should pack their bags, go home and "get on with their lives".

Two years earlier John Howard had wrongly accused Iraqi asylum seekers of throwing their children overboard. He now prepared to accuse the Nauru Afghans of starving their own children for reasons of a similar kind. When a rumour began to circulate that the hunger strikers were encouraging their children to join in, the ultra-sensitive ears of the Prime Minister pricked up. He ordered an immediate investigation into whether or not the reports were true. Of this matter no more was heard. As it turned out, the rumours were completely false.

Hypocrisy was once described as the compliment vice pays to virtue. In the response of the Australian government to the Nauru hunger strike there was no hypocrisy. No one bothered even to pretend to care about whether the hunger strikers lived or died.

On the eighth and ninth days of the hunger strike a UNHCR delegation came on a pre-arranged visit to Nauru. Among the hunger strikers there was bitter disappointment. "They did nothing," Elaine Smith was informed. In fact the Canberra office of UNHCR seems to have become deeply worried. After the visit to Nauru it warned of an impending "human tragedy". On Christmas Eve it announced that it intended to re-open the cases of twenty-two Nauru Afghans it had originally rejected. It was re-opening these cases, it stressed, not because of the hunger strike but because of the deteriorating security situation in Afghanistan. This decision finally prompted a response from Australia. The Minister for Immigration announced that as soon as new UNHCR information on Afghanistan was produced, "the Government will examine the implications for those cases on Nauru previously assessed by DIMIA."

Despite these promises, the strike continued for another fortnight. For inscrutable reasons of his own, on 6 January the Nauruan Finance Minister criticised the indifference of the Australian government to the hunger strikers and to the pressure this indifference had placed on the health system of Nauru. Shortly after, he issued an invitation to an independent team of Australian doctors, under the auspices of the AMA, who had offered Nauru medical advice and assistance. Those who had gone on hunger strike did not wish to die. What they wanted was a human life. In combination, the UNHCR initiative and the invitation to the Australian doctors seems to have convinced the strikers that at least something had been achieved. They were no longer altogether abandoned and totally forgotten. The strike ended without death, although the long-term health of many was uncertain. One striker, it was said, had gone completely mad.

Nothing on Nauru is simple. Nauru's threat to allow an independent medical team onto the island, which would effectively have ended Australia's ban on non-official visits, stirred the Australian government to action. It offered now to send an official team of its own to assess Nauru's medical needs. For its part Nauru made clear it no longer wished the non-official medical team to come. On Topside the atmosphere was now confused and apprehensive, although not entirely without hope. It was unclear what, if anything, had been gained by the hunger strike.

> Nothing should grow unless planted, and whatever would have grown on its own must have been the wrong thing … What was needed … was the posture, and skills, of a gardener; one armed with a detailed design of the lawn, of the borders and of the furrows dividing the lawn from the borders … with determination to treat as weeds every self-invited plant …
>
> —Zygmunt Bauman on the nature of "modernity"

Australian asylum seeker policy was long preoccupied with the search for a deterrent system which worked. By August 2001 it was clear that mandatory detention and temporary protection had failed. During 2002, however, it gradually became obvious that the successor measures – the plausible threats of military repulsion and Pacific island incarceration – actually worked. A year after Operation Relex had been mounted and the Pacific Solution put in place, not one asylum seeker boat had arrived. Having found an effective deterrent, the attention of the government and Immigration Minister now shifted to a different policy challenge – how to send the fourth-wave asylum seekers home. With regard to the realisation of this ambition, each of the three main countries from which the asylum seekers had fled – Afghanistan, Iran and Iraq – posed a different political problem.

The brightest prospect for large-scale repatriation was Afghanistan where, in early 2002, the Taliban had been overthrown by a US-led, UN-backed military coalition. The logic of the Australian government's position on the asylum seeker front was simple. The Afghan asylum seekers had told Australia they had fled from the Taliban. The Taliban had been toppled. The Afghan asylum seekers should now go home. Of course it was true that the situation of these asylum seekers varied. Most were now in Australia, accepted as genuine refugees but on three-year temporary protection visas, which would soon expire. A small number had been languishing for years, as rejectees, in one or another Australian detention centre. Several hundred who had been rescued by the *Tampa* or had tried to reach Australia soon after, who had fled from the Taliban regime but whose refugee claims had been assessed after its overthrow, were by now marooned on Nauru, most but not all as UNHCR or Department of Immigration rejectees. No matter whether they were in Australia or on Nauru, no matter whether they were refugees or rejectees, the Australian government now hoped eventually to send all the Afghan asylum seekers home.

In May 2002 the Immigration Minister flew to Kabul to sign a Memorandum of Understanding with the Afghan Interim Administration. Ruddock described its aim as "voluntary return, with dignity and in safety, for Afghans who do not engage Australia's protection obligations". At the time a spokesman warned that although voluntary return was desired and anticipated, "at some point in the future" force might have to be used. Shortly after the signature of the Memorandum of Understanding, the first Australian "reintegration package" was announced. As we have seen, $2000 was to be paid to an individual and $10,000 to a family if they were willing to go home. In addition, "a range of support services" was to be provided to help the returnees re-establish their lives. Detainees in Australia and on Nauru were given twenty-eight days to decide.

In mid-2002 the government claimed there was no intention of offering the repatriation package to the TPV refugees. In December that decision was reversed. As we have seen, many Afghan TPVs were deeply disturbed on receipt of a letter which they interpreted as part of an ongoing government campaign to force them to leave. Some believe that the arrival of this letter marked a critical moment in Dr Habib's disintegration. All TPV holders were given six months to decide whether or not to accept the money on offer, which they were told was estimated to be five times the annual income of the average Afghan. Of the 3400 or so Afghans to whom the offer was sent, thirty-three (fewer than 1 per cent) eventually agreed.

The TPV repatriation letter coincided with an extraordinarily tendentious Australian government assessment of the situation inside Afghanistan, entitled *Events in the Islamic Transitional Government in Afghanistan*. By the time of its publication security in post-Taliban Afghanistan was already deteriorating, as seen in the absence of central administration control beyond Kabul; the restoration of warlord rule; the return of many of the complex ethnic-religious-political localised conflicts of the past; and even the revival in some parts of Afghanistan of Taliban power. All of this was ignored. When Australia's foremost expert on contemporary Afghanistan, William Maley, read the Australian assessment, he could scarcely believe his eyes. It did not even analyse regional situations separately. "I regret to say that my overall view is ... that, given the reliance that a Temporary Protection Visa holder might place on *Events in the Islamic Transitional Government of Afghanistan*, the document should be regarded not simply as misleading, but as highly irresponsible."

In July 2002 both of the key international bodies, UNHCR and IOM, announced that the time had come for Afghan refugees, at "whatever stage they may be in the asylum process", to return to their homeland. UNHCR was chiefly interested in speeding the return of the three million or so Afghans in the neighbouring countries of Pakistan and Iran. The Australian government was delighted by this announcement. Others, however, like Médicins sans Frontières, who understood the fragility of the situation on the ground, were dismayed. Its program director, Pierre Salignon, argued: "I think it's dangerous to have this kind of statement in so unstable a situation."

Salignon was proved right. UNHCR optimism eroded steadily over the next eighteen months. In mid-2003 the head of the UNHCR's Kabul office, Phillipe Leclerc, visited Australia. He claimed there was now a near-complete absence in Afghanistan of the rule of law. In September 2003 the Secretary-General of the United Nations, Kofi Annan, warned: "Arbitrary rule by local commanders prevails in many areas of the country ... In the south and south-east, this insecurity is greatly exacerbated by the activities of the Taliban and other insurgents." In November a UNHCR official, Bettina Goislard, was shot dead in the province of Ghazni, from which many of the Hazaras in Australia or on Nauru had fled. UNHCR now closed all offices in Kandahar, Helmand, Paktia, Patkika, Khost, Kunar, Laghman and Nangarhar. It suspended repatriation from Pakistan. At the same time Canada extended its decision not to repatriate Afghans for another six months. In December 2003 Kofi Annan went so far as to warn that unless the security situation improved, "we may lose Afghanistan."

None of this had the slightest impact on the repatriation program of the Australian government. Quite the contrary. Recently some extraordinary evidence on this matter came to light on ABC television. In 2002 Andrew Wilkie, a senior analyst at the Office of National Assessments, one of Australia's most significant intelligence agencies, was asked to produce a report on the security situation inside post-Taliban Afghanistan. Wilkie explained what happened then:

> It was quite a damning assessment. The prognosis I developed was
> that the situation was dire and likely to stay that way for the fore-
> seeable future. But, in fact, the senior management of the Office of
> National Assessments said that that assessment would not go out
> because it was just such a political hot potato to be saying that at
> the time the Government was saying publicly that it would start the
> return of the asylum seekers.

Wilkie protested the decision of the ONA's Director-General, Kim Jones. Eventually a "watered-down" version was sent. At stake in matters of this kind were the lives of human beings.

From Australia during 2003 some forty Afghan rejectees decided to go home. The reason was not difficult to grasp: "I spent three years in detention," Daulat Khan explained, "I was not prepared to stay there and rot and go mad like the rest of them." From Nauru in November and December 2003 two planeloads of Afghans were returned to Kabul. Throughout

2003 smaller repatriations from Nauru occurred at regular intervals. Many returned precisely because of the remorseless pressure placed upon them by the Department of Immigration and IOM. "At first", a Nauruan Afghan wrote to an Australian friend, "no one wrote their names for deportation but your government compelled us and put pressure on us to return ... DIMIA came every week and said to us", that if you do not depart voluntarily, "we will send you by force." The Nauruan Afghans returned although they had been warned repeatedly by earlier detainees of the dangers they would face. "After 20 days", one wrote, quite typically, "we were compelled to leave Kabul ... We were afraid of going back to our villages and cities. Most of us couldn't find our families ... Some went to other cities, some went to Iran, and I with eleven other refugees came to Peshawar [in Pakistan] ..."

On 30 November 2003 − after the closure of the UNHCR offices in Ghazni, after the Canadian repatriation decision − Australia sent a further twenty-two Nauruan Afghans to Kabul. In the Senate the new Immigration Minister, Amanda Vanstone, was asked about the dangers they might face. At first she admitted entire ignorance of the situation. She then added the following words. "Australia does not repatriate people if we believe there is a risk to them − an inappropriate risk. I mean, there is a risk in walking across the street, obviously."

One of the first Afghans who returned from Nauru was Mohammad Mussa Nazari. He came from a relatively prosperous Hazara farming family from the Malistan district of Ghazni province. Like so many of the Hazara, Mussa fled from the Taliban in the late 1990s, leaving behind his wife and children, his parents and his brothers. Mussa was one of those Hazaras who sought asylum in Australia after the *Tampa* rescue. The boat on which he came was impounded by the Navy during Operation Relex. First he was detained on Christmas Island and then sent on to Nauru. Because of the dreadful conditions in the Nauru camps, because of his objectively hopeless situation as a post-Taliban rejectee, and because he seems to have believed what the Department of Immigration told him about the supposedly improved security situation in Afghanistan, Mussa accepted the Australian reintegration package. He was on the November 2002 flight to Kabul. We asked his brother, who is now in Malistan, why Mussa had returned. "He was told that your country is safe now and … that you should apply because it is okay to go back … And also because he was tired, he came back." Mussa returned to the family's farm.

One morning in August 2003 Mussa left his home to open a pond to water the fields. The family's land is adjacent to Pashtun territory. Mussa was accompanied by a Hazara friend, Jafar. On their way home, on Jafar's motorbike, the pair were ambushed. Both were murdered. Mussa was shot through the top of his head. The motorbike was stolen.

We asked Mussa's brother why he thought Mussa had been killed. In part he blamed the death on renewed ethnic and religious conflict between the Pashtuns and the Hazaras. He told us the Malistan Hazaras once more live in fear. No one has yet investigated the murder; the Hazaras are too frightened to ask for an inquiry by the local Pashtuns, who are in control. He claimed that there existed in Malistan no effective government, only "corruption" everywhere. He also claimed that Mussa's local fame or notoriety, as a returnee who had tried to reach the West, also made him vulnerable. He told us he believed it was altogether wrong, in the circumstances, for his brother to have been pressed by the Australian government to go home. "I don't believe people who return here will be safe."

At first Canberra doubted whether Mussa's murder had even taken place. Later it regarded the motivation for the murder as clear. "This person", Senator Vanstone explained, "was found not to be a refugee and this decision was upheld after a full merits review. He chose to go home voluntarily. His death in a robbery almost a year later is tragic but casts no doubt on the reliability of his refugee determination."

How far Mussa's murder is attributable to local ethnic and religious tensions; how far to a generalised lawlessness; how far to a combination of both, we are unable to say. Of only one thing are we sure. Canberra's description of contemporary Afghanistan as "safe and secure" for the return of asylum seekers is ignorant at best and at worst an outright lie.

For the five hundred or so Afghans who have been repatriated thus far, the situation has not, of course, turned out as tragically as it did for Mussa Nazari. A more typical story is that of Hassan, to whom we spoke in the preparation of this essay.

Hassan was rejected by Australia as a refugee on the grounds that he came not from Afghanistan but Pakistan. As it turned out, this was false. When the migration agent Marion Le was in a village of Afghanistan on other business she was approached by Hassan's brother. Nevertheless the Minister refused to re-open his case. Hassan knew he was going mad in prolonged detention. He decided to accept the repatriation package and take his chances at home.

For a month he was overjoyed to be in Afghanistan with his wife and the young child he hardly knew. Soon he realised that the perilous local political situation from which he had escaped was in essence unchanged. "I have enemies in Afghanistan," he told us. It was from these enemies that within a month of his arrival he was, once again, to flee.

We spoke to Hassan in Quetta, Pakistan. He was again without his wife and child. Although Quetta is less dangerous, he told us, it also is not safe. There is anti-Shia and anti-Hazara prejudice and violence. The Taliban is regrouping. He is keeping a low profile. Nor has he recovered from the detention experience in Australia. "Basically", he told us, "I am mentally disturbed." He suffers chronic anxiety and depression but has no access to the medication on which, in Australian detention, he had come to rely. Not everyone doubts that he is a genuine refugee. In Quetta, Hassan is once again being assisted by UNHCR.

The Howard government has become rather wary about sending Afghan detainees home. Recently, some of those who had agreed to return as early as mid-2002 were told that now they could leave only if they signed a document releasing Australia from responsibility for their fate in Afghanistan. We have been told that one man who did sign is now very "distressed" and has left Afghanistan for Pakistan. We have also been told that another potential returnee who "volunteered" has refused to sign and remains in detention.

Iran provided far fewer fourth-wave asylum seekers than did Afghanistan or Iraq. It also provided the largest number of asylum seekers who were rejected as refugees. While more than 450 Iranians were eventually granted temporary protection visas, in February 2004 160 remained in detention. Most of these people had been detained for several years. Two had been in prison-like conditions for five. Of these long-term Iranian detainees a very small number have voluntarily returned to Iran. One reason for this is obvious. Of the three main countries from which the fourth-wave asylum seekers fled, Iran is the only one which has not experienced "regime change". Although in recent years there have been occasional signs of moderate liberalisation (in February 2004 seemingly suffering reverse), Iran remains an intact theocratic secret-police state. The Iranian regime enforces religious orthodoxy, heavily censors free speech, regularly imprisons, tortures and executes serious internal political opponents. In 2002 the US Department of State described the human rights situation in contemporary Iran in the following words:

> Systematic abuses include summary executions, disappearances, widespread use of torture and other degrading treatment, reportedly including rape, severe punishments such as stoning and flogging, harsh prison conditions, arbitrary arrest and detention, and prolonged and incommunicado detention ...

Some of the long-term Iranian detainees are members of dissident political parties. Some are Christian converts or pre-Christian Mandaeans or members of smaller religious sects. Some are members of ethnic minorities – Arabs or Kurds. The obvious reason why such people have refused to return voluntarily to Iran is that they still are frightened of the regime from which they fled. A more complex additional reason is that the system of long-term detention has so broken the spirit and paralysed the will of its victims that, gradually, they have lost the capacity to choose or to act.

One of the most tragic elements of the entire fourth-wave asylum seeker story is the stalemate that has developed in the relations between the Australian government and the long-term Iranian detainees, and the cat-and-mouse games with the lives of those people that the government has, over the past year, begun to play.

In March 2003 the Minister for Immigration announced that he had signed a Memorandum of Understanding with the Iranian government for the repatriation of all the rejected asylum seekers from Iran. According to the announcement, while the government's "first priority" was voluntary returns, "arrangements for the handling of those who do not volunteer ... have also been established." There was at the time considerable scepticism about this announcement. Asylum seekers had learned not to trust anything the government said. Refugee advocates did not believe that Iran would sign an agreement which would create a precedent for non-voluntary repatriation. Europe currently has large numbers of Iranian asylum seekers; Iran has always strenuously opposed their forcible return. As the Refugee Council of Australia explained, if Iran "were to accept the 190 or so failed asylum seekers from Australia, it would be hard for it to resist the effort from European states to return the tens of thousands of Iranian asylum seekers there".

In the face of this scepticism it would appear that the government decided to leak a draft of the Memorandum of Understanding, which had within it provisions for forcible return. Julie Macken of the *Australian Financial Review* raised the issue with the Iranian Embassy in Canberra. She received from it the following, curious reply. On the one hand, "Iran does not want involuntary repatriation." On the other, "If the Australian government put Iranians on a plane and dumped them on our tarmac, obviously we would not reject them." For his part, the Minister brushed aside any suggestion even of Iranian ambiguity over the question of non-voluntary return. The agreement was clear. If Iran wanted to keep its details confidential that was only because of the foreign policy "implications", "that is their dealings with other governments".

By now the head of the UN Working Group on Arbitrary Detention, Louis Joinet, who had visited Australia in the previous year, was greatly concerned. It seemed to be the case that the Australian–Iranian agreement for involuntary repatriation contained no mechanism for guaranteeing the safety of the Iranian returnees. As these people might, self-evidently, face persecution, why had the United Nations High Commission for Refugees, which had the capacity to monitor their situations, not been involved in the negotiation of the Memorandum?

The Minister responded to Joinet's question with a legal-bureaucratic formula of a characteristic kind. "Individuals are not removed where this would place Australia in breach of its international obligations." His Departmental Secretary claimed that "our system" has discovered that the Iranians "do not have any reason to fear returning". How our system had discovered this was left unexplained. According to the Minister, Australia respected the international principles both of non-*refoulement* (that is, the transfer to situations of danger of individuals threatened with persecution) and of non-interference in the affairs of sovereign states. That these principles might be in tension or even in conflict in the case of the involuntary return of the Iranian asylum seekers was something the Minister was altogether unprepared to concede.

At the time the draft Memorandum of Understanding was leaked, so too was a significant departmental minute. The minute was written by a senior public servant, John Okely, in December 2002. It provided outsiders with a rare insight into the way Immigration Department officials had, by now quite unselfconsciously, come to think. "The Department's experience suggests", the minute argued, "that for all hardcore detainees, the key to ensuring voluntary departure lies in the creation of a credible threat of involuntary removal." Previously, Okely pointed out, the Department had advised against the offer of a financial package "until it is clear that the Iranian authorities will co-operate in involuntary removals if required". Okely suggested a policy of "targetting" for involuntary repatriation a group he called "emergency cases", which comprised, in particular, those "who have attempted self-harm or committed acts of violence within the centres". Because of the "public embarrassment" their behaviour caused the government of Iran, the Iranians had indicated that they might support their forcible removal. In turn, the involuntary removal of "difficult detainees, irrespective of the number, is likely to make it easier for others to choose to depart voluntarily". Rarely has the ruthless cynicism of the Department of Immigration, in its dealings with asylum seekers, been outlined with greater clarity.

In late April 2003 the Department moved into action, along the lines suggested by Okely. A familiar reintegration package was now offered to all Iranian detainees. It was accompanied by an open and less familiar threat. "If you choose not to accept voluntary return within 28 days, plans for your involuntary removal will begin and you will be removed from Australia as soon as practicable without the benefits of financial assistance."

This letter occasioned considerable panic among the Iranian detainees, as it was meant to do. One man, who had by now lost his mind, slashed himself as he had often done before on the arrival of unsettling news. In the longer term, however, very few Iranians responded to the threats as the Department had hoped. By August only fifteen reintegration acceptances had arrived. The press now reported that the forcible removals were about to begin. In their despair, the detainees wrote an open letter to the Prime Minister and people of Australia. "It is Friday night and we are all very frightened because they tell us that tomorrow we will be deported by force ... we are too afraid of the torture and the prison we will have to go to ..." The cries of the detainees, it need hardly be said, fell on indifferent and determinedly deaf ears.

In late August three men were taken from the Baxter detention centre. One was able to remain in Australia because of legal action. The other two were removed. At Perth airport both were told that if they signed a Department of Immigration document they would receive $700. At least one of the men signed, although he did not know what the document contained. On the flight back to Iran one had to be physically restrained. As the Minister explained in his characteristic cadence: "If people behave in ways that are likely to jeopardise the safe travel of passengers, those matters need to be properly addressed." In accordance with the Okely strategy, the threat of force had been used to encourage voluntary return. At once the Department sent the intransigent detainees a new and final bargain-basement offer – $1000 per person; $5000 per family; an acceptance deadline of fourteen days. For a second time there was almost no response.

On behalf of the detainees, instead, ill-fated legal actions were now mounted to try to prevent the government from continuing with its threat of further forcible repatriation. In mid-December 2003, in a similar case concerning an Algerian, a judgement of the Full Federal Court pointed out, with almost disarming frankness, that "even if it is virtually certain that he or she will be killed, tortured or persecuted in that country, whether on Refugee Convention grounds or not, that is not a practical consideration going to the ability to remove from Australia". In contemporary Australia, in other words, it is lawful for a government to send an asylum seeker to their predictable death.

Some of the Iranian detainees are extremely well-informed about events at home. After the forcible Baxter deportations two Iranian detainees gathered considerable information about what had happened to these two deportees. Their accounts were passed to an Iranian at Villawood. From them he produced two statutory declarations. Both are in our possession. What follows is what they claim.

We shall call the two men who were forcibly deported Ali and Shahin. Each man travelled to Dubai with two non-uniformed guards and from Dubai to Tehran with two new guards. On arrival they were greeted by officials of the Iranian Information and Intelligence Agency. They were separated.

Ali went first to an interrogation room and then to a room where an official of the Australian Embassy was waiting. As instructed, he said that he had experienced no problems and was, indeed, happy to be back in Iran. Ali returned to the interrogation room. He was asked to supply information about a list of Iranians held in Australian detention – their behaviour, their religious beliefs and so on. Having assured the security officials he had not converted to Christianity, Ali was released. He is said, in the statutory declaration, to be living now far from Tehran and in fear.

Unlike Ali, or so it is claimed, on his return from initial interrogation Shahin informed the Australian officials that he did indeed have problems with the Iranian government. Unlike Ali he was not released. According to the statutory declaration, he was taken, as his brother before him had been, to the notorious Evin prison, where he was "beaten, tortured and interrogated severely" and, after a fortnight, released on bail.

We do not know whether or not the stories in the statutory declarations are true. They are said to have been told to the author of the documents by two separate people both of whom had spoken to the men concerned. If the account of what has happened to Ali and Shahin is mistaken or even mischievous, the government should reveal what it knows about their fate. If, alternatively, out of respect for Iranian sovereignty it has not investigated what has happened and knows nothing, it should explain why it believes the fate of returnees it has forcibly removed is a matter with which it need not be concerned.

It should also tell us whether it is concerned with the fate of some of the Iranians who have "voluntarily" returned. One of these is a man we shall call Jamal, a long-term Port Hedland detainee, who attempted suicide at Easter in 2003 and who was told about his impending removal while still in solitary confinement following unrest at the Port Hedland centre in late 2003. On his arrival at Tehran, or so we have been told, a baptismal certificate was discovered in Jamal's bags. He was held at the airport for nine days and then released. He is now waiting for a court hearing. With reason, he is afraid. We have been informed by Australian witnesses we regard as reliable that a few years ago two previous Iranian returnees were charged with religious offences – one for conversion to Bahai, the other for conversion to Christianity. The alleged Bahai convert has not been heard of since. The Christian convert received a sentence of twenty-five years' imprisonment. It is to this perilous and unpredictable world that the Iranian detainees will return.

Perhaps in Canberra this is now beginning to be acknowledged. As Russell Skelton pointed out in the *Age* of 16 February 2004, the cases of some forty Sabian Mandaeans in detention are presently under "review". He also reported that while in his final ten months of office Philip Ruddock granted only eighteen protection visas to long-term Iranian detainees, since October 2003 his successor, Senator Amanda Vanstone, has granted visas to forty-three Iranians. Even more promisingly, according to an Immigration spokesperson Senator Vanstone has now abandoned Philip Ruddock's unconscionable program for the involuntary repatriation of long-term Iranian detainees. There are grounds here for hope.

Among the fourth-wave asylum seekers, Iraqis have, so far, proven to be the most difficult group to send home. Virtually all the Iraqi asylum seekers who reached Australia were eventually found to be genuine refugees and granted temporary protection visas. Those few Iraqi cases which failed concerned, in general, people who were deemed to have abandoned situations of effective protection offered them elsewhere.

Before the demise of Saddam Hussein's regime, with the fall of Baghdad in May 2003, the repatriation to Iraq of failed asylum seekers, let alone of refugees, was morally unthinkable. After the regime had been militarily overthrown – because of general insecurity, infrastructural collapse and the near-total breakdown of law and order – UNHCR warned repeatedly against premature programs of repatriation. Indeed in July 2003 it warned that the return of large numbers of Iraqi asylum seekers might not be possible before 2005.

With regard to the Iraqi rejectees on Nauru, Australia simply ignored this advice. After May 2003 twenty-three were successfully pressed to go home. With regard, however, to the long-term Iraqi detainees in Australia the advice was, more or less, accepted. At a time when the Department of Immigration was threatening Iranian detainees with forcible repatriation if they did not volunteer to go home, it adopted a neutral policy towards their Iraqi equivalents, neither encouraging nor discouraging their voluntary return. The handful of Iraqi detainees who agreed to go home after the fall of Saddam were people for whom the present horrors of detention in Australia outweighed whatever future fears they might have about the chaos and violence of occupied Iraq. In this sense, and this sense alone, they were genuine "volunteers".

Hussein is a typical case. On his way to Australia he was described by a friend to whom we have spoken as a normal man, quiet, co-operative, even cheerful. During his detention at Woomera all this changed. Hussein was involved in serious unrest and spent several periods in jail. He inflicted wounds upon himself, threatened suicide, lost all self-control. On one occasion, we were told, when his friend rang him Hussein wept for several minutes. He was, in short, a not unusual product of the mandatory detention system – a broken man.

After three years in detention, when Saddam was still in power, Hussein began demanding to be sent home. The coming of war did not change his resolve. Eventually the Department agreed. Accompanied by an Australian, Hussein flew to Singapore on an Australian Travel Document, supplied by the Department of Foreign Affairs, and with a Syrian visa. In Dubai he struck trouble. Emirates officials had suspicions about his documentation. The Australian Embassy in Dubai became involved. It offered to help Hussein return to Australia. He absolutely refused. He would go anywhere but Australia. For more than two weeks Hussein was stranded at Dubai airport, in detention. Eventually his lawyer in Australia made contact with the UNHCR office in Egypt. He was taken to Jordan and, with a group of Iraqi returnees, driven from the border to Baghdad. The city frightened him.

He described to his friend the smoke and the explosions. Hussein soon decided to return to his home village.

In late December 2003, like Hussein, the entire Kadem family volunteered to return to Iraq. By that time the family had been almost entirely destroyed by their experiences in Australia. Different members of the family – husband, wife, four sons and two young daughters – had spent considerable stretches of time at Curtin, Port Hedland, Maribyrnong, Perth airport detention centre, Perth jail. The father and the sons had been involved in riots, hunger strikes and suicide attempts. The father, Abdul, had spent a year in jail after pleading guilty to having acted as an interpreter for a people smuggler. His wife, Ban, who had been transferred with her children to Maribyrnong, was so seriously depressed that even the Department of Immigration had felt obliged to release her into the community on a bridging visa, which meant that she relied on voluntary organisations to supply her most basic needs. Worst of all was the condition of one of the sons, Mohammed. He had been introduced to hard drugs at Maribyrnong – where criminals awaiting deportation are also held – and had developed an addiction. He also suffered from the early symptoms of psychosis.

Abdul Kadem, a proud and extremely angry man, was desperate to leave Australia. At first he tried, unsuccessfully, to get his family to Syria and Indonesia and then, successfully, to Vietnam. News of the family had reached authorities there. They were turned around at the airport and deported, via Thailand, back to detention in Australia. In October 2003 Abdul Kadem gave up and volunteered to "return" to Iraq, a country he had left some thirteen years before. The Department of Immigration advanced the family an ex gratia payment of $7000, undoubtedly glad to be rid of the Kadems.

Surrounded by a team of Australian and then Jordanian guards, two Immigration officials and a nurse, the family was flown to Jordan. The family was taken by car to the Iraqi border. After the payment of appropriate bribes, the Kadems were handed over to drivers to take them to their relations in Baghdad. When telephoned, these relations were astonished to hear that the Kadem family were alone in lawless Baghdad in the middle of the night.

We have spoken to family members on a number of occasions since their return. Electricity, gas and petrol are scarcely available. Because of omnipresent violent street crime they say it is difficult to leave home, even in the middle of the day. The sound of gunfire and of explosions can be heard at all times. Half an hour after Ban visited a clinic, she learned that it had been destroyed by a bomb. She does not know why. Her sons were staying with their maternal grandmother when American troops, searching for insurgents, burst into a neighbouring apartment, killing three. Last time we spoke, Mohammed, who is in general in a terrible condition, had taken an overdose of painkillers and had almost died. The hospitals in Baghdad, they told us, are like "garages". The father is at present making preparations to take his family to Iran. Like very many returnees from detention his hatred for the Australian government is fierce.

Shortly after the invasion of Iraq the Minister for Immigration spoke about paying Iraqis to go home some time in the future. His spokesperson shortly added that this might be possible in a matter of months. The Minister pointed out that the new political situation would clearly affect Iraqis' eligibility for further protection. No doubt some would like to claim they are still refugees, "whatever regime emerges in future". If so, they were likely to be disappointed. "Changed circumstances may well be relevant in determining", he warned, "whether a temporary visa would be renewed."

Throughout 2003, because of the calamitous situation on the ground in Iraq – so dangerous that even the hardened officials of the International Organisation of Migration refused to travel there or to assist in the repatriation unless given legal immunity by the returnee – the Department froze all consideration of temporary protection visa renewal for Iraqi refugees. There can be little doubt, however, that when the Department comes to consider Iraq even moderately safe its ultimate hope of being able to repatriate the four thousand or more Iraqis on temporary protection visas will revive.

It seems unlikely that, in October 1999, the introduction of temporary protection visas was seen by the Department of Immigration as an instrument for sending the fourth-wave asylum seekers home. According to the October 1999 regulations TPV holders would gain permanent protection if, in three years' time, they could still prove their need for protection. The events of September 11 and their geopolitical consequences were still in the future. No one could yet have imagined that the regimes from which the overwhelming majority of the fourth-wave asylum seekers had fled – Afghanistan and Iraq – would both be overthrown by military force before the temporary protection visas had expired. Through "reintegration" packages, the Department of Immigration has, thus far, been able to send home some six hundred fourth-wave asylum seekers from Australia and Nauru. With the toppling of the Taliban and Saddam Hussein, the temporary protection visa system provided the Australian government with a splendid, unanticipated opportunity to send eight thousand Afghan and Iraqi refugees home.

The legal process by which this outcome might be achieved can be outlined very briefly. Each application for a further protection visa will follow the same legal course as the original application, with two differences. Whether permanency can be given will be determined by the 27 September 2001 ruling. If an appeal under Section 417 to the Minister fails, the refugee will either be removed from Australia or, if that proves impossible, will be returned to mandatory detention.

Almost five hundred Afghan cases for visa renewal have already been heard. Of the 495 primary decisions that have been given, eleven cases have succeeded and 484 have failed. However, the Refugee Review Tribunal's twenty-eight decisions on these rejected Afghan cases have so far favoured the protection claims four to one. It is not impossible that future Afghan primary decisions will be more favourable to the applicants, in part because of new UNHCR information about the situation inside Afghanistan and in part because the Department might become uneasy if too high a proportion of its Afghan primary decisions are overturned. In a recent hearing a Tribunal member, Dr Mirko Bargaric, argued that as there were no "permanent state structures in Afghanistan", it was difficult to accept that changes to the political situation were permanent. This may be a sign of things to come.

Almost no non-Afghan further protection primary decisions have yet been made. Because of the perilous and uncertain situation on the ground in Iraq, the Department has frozen (or as it prefers to say, deferred) consideration of further Iraqi cases. It is hard to see how, if their cases are soon unfrozen, the Iraqis' claims could succeed.

The situation can perhaps be summarised like this. While most Iranian cases for further protection visas seem likely to succeed as there has been no regime change in Iran, many of the Afghan cases and almost all of the Iraqi cases will most probably fail. If so, in two years' time, thousands of Afghan or Iraqi refugees, who have spent five or six years in Australia, may either be in detention once more or have been successfully despatched to the new perils and chaos of the countries from which once they fled.

> The quality of mercy is not strain'd,
> It droppeth as the gentle rain from heaven
> Upon the place beneath; it is twice bless'd;
> It blesseth him that gives and him that takes.
>
> —Shakespeare, *The Merchant of Venice*

The United Nations Refugee Convention of 1951 is one of the great achievements of the generation which lived through the terrible breakdown of European civilisation in the period between the beginning of the First and the end of the Second World War. This generation was deeply affected by memories of the betrayal of the Jews of Central Europe who, before the implementation of the Nazi Final Solution, could not find countries which would offer them asylum. It was also affected by the vast problem of millions of displaced persons in post-war Europe who had been driven from their homes by war, revolution and the imposition throughout Eastern Europe of Stalinist rule. The UN Convention forbade the *refoulement* of anyone with a well-founded fear of persecution because of their race, religion, nationality, political opinions or membership of a social group. Those who signed the Convention committed themselves to providing such refugees, one way or another, with protection from the persecution they had fled.

In recent years the UN Refugee Convention has come, increasingly, under threat. A huge gulf has opened between the letter of refugee law and the spirit in which it is now applied. The Western countries who have signed the Convention are committed to making some form of assessment of the claims of every asylum seeker who arrives at their border, and to offering some form of protection to every asylum seeker whose refugee claim they assess to be genuine. Nevertheless there is now no Western country whose behaviour is consistent with the spirit which animated the UN Convention at the time of its creation. According to the standard hypocrisy now surrounding refugee administration and law, all Western countries try to prevent the arrival on their territory of asylum seekers whose protection claims, if their deterrence measures fail, they then solemnly assess. It is as if a government which at one stage constructed a secure and comfortable refuge for the protection of women who had been brutally assaulted, at a later time decided to surround it with fierce guard dogs and razor wire to prevent victims from making it to the door.

There are two main reasons for the retreat within the West from the spirit of the Refugee Convention. The Cold War provided an unusually propitious climate for refugees, or at least for those fleeing from communist regimes to the West. The Cold War was a time of struggle for supremacy between the Western capitalist and Soviet communist worlds. The refugees from communism had voted with their feet. Their flight was regarded as evidence of Western political, economic and moral superiority. Although European anti-communist refugees were especially welcome – for example those who fled from the Soviet invasions of Hungary in 1956 and of Czechoslovakia in 1968 – the benign influence of Cold War competition on refugees was also seen in the willingness of a number of Western governments to settle ungrumblingly hundreds of thousands of Indochinese refugees after the communist victories of 1975.

Since the end of the Cold War, Islamic terrorism or fundamentalist Islam has gradually become the new enemy of the West. However, because there exists no global competition for supremacy between the West and Islam (the West's superiority being simply assumed), refugees from Islamic regimes have never come to be regarded with the kind of ideological favour anti-communist refugees experienced in the previous historical era.

This is not the only reason for the decline of sympathy for refugees throughout the West. Over time the mobility of non-Western peoples has increased, as has the gap in material standards between Western and non-Western societies. In Europe and North America very large numbers of people from both the non-Western and post-communist worlds have sought residence in the West through the exploitation of existing refugee law, that is by claims of persecution which are either exaggerated or invented. In the West, as a consequence, the term asylum seeker has acquired a distinctly pejorative edge. In such an atmosphere the vital distinction between those who claim asylum to improve their material lot and those who have fled from savage tyrannies has been weakened or lost. In the West, anti-asylum seeker rhetoric has become a staple of populist politics. In the West, as well, systems to deter asylum seeker have been constructed. These systems do not discriminate between those whose asylum claims are weak and those whose claims are as strong as any refugee claim has ever been.

The Australian variant of this general pattern is rather strange. There is hardly a Western country where there has been a smaller number of asylum seekers than Australia. There is hardly a Western country where the percentage of genuine asylum seeker claims has been higher. Since the Second World War the largest wave of spontaneous asylum seeker arrivals were the 9500 boat people who reached the northern Australian coastline between 1999 and 2001. As we have seen, the overwhelming majority of these asylum seekers had fled from two of the most vicious tyrannies on earth – Iraq under Saddam Hussein and Afghanistan under the Taliban. A smaller number had fled from the theocratic police state of Iran. Given the political circumstances from which these people had fled, it is hardly surprising that more than 90 per cent were discovered by Australia's stringent processing system to be genuine refugees.

We arrive now at the fundamental paradox of asylum seeker politics in Australia – the discrepancy between the smallness of the size of the asylum seeker "problem" and the height of the anti-asylum seeker wall. Between 1989 and 1992 Australia introduced a unique system of mandatory detention for all asylum seekers, that is for the automatic, indiscriminate, indefinite and judicially unreviewable imprisonment of all asylum seekers either until they have been removed from Australia or have proved their refugee claims to be true. Between 1999 and 2001 it introduced, even for those genuine refugees, a unique and increasingly rigid system of mere temporary protection. And in 2001 it began to use military force to drive all asylum seekers back to the country from which their boats had set sail or, failing that, to transport all those who fell under Australia's control to offshore Pacific island processing camps where their claims were to be assessed. Although by Western standards only very small numbers of asylum seekers have ever reached Australia; although almost all those reaching Australia recently have been genuine refugees, Australia has created the most formidable anti-asylum seeker deterrent system of any country in the world.

If signatories to the UN Convention were to follow Australia's example, no asylum seeker fleeing a Third World tyranny – other than those arriving with valid visas – would ever reach any Western country. If, moreover, non-signatories were to follow Australia's lead, by using military force to prevent all border crossing, there would be no means of escape at all. Australia is, in other words, the pioneer of an anti-asylum seeker system whose replication by other countries would destroy one of the finest achievements of post-war liberal civilisation – the offer of protection for those who are fleeing from tyranny.

According to a recent estimate there are fourteen million refugees in the world today and an additional eight million people of "concern" to the United Nations High Commission for Refugees. Given the magnitude of the refugee problem, why should Australia behave generously towards those twelve thousand who reached or tried to reach Australian territory between 1999 and 2001? This is a fundamental question which we would answer in the following way.

Let us imagine that a woman who has been savagely attacked arrived at our door appealing for help. Let us imagine, in addition, that we answered her with the following words: "We understand the difficulties that you face, but you must understand ours. Do you not realise that there are, in this city, thousands of women who have been in a situation like yours? If we offered you help, which we are, of course, sorely tempted to do, is it not obvious that news would soon spread beyond this neighbourhood that when it comes to women in your position, we are a soft touch? No doubt others would soon turn up at our door. Where would it all end? We noticed, by the way, that you arrived in an unlicensed taxi. Many of the women from the poorer neighbourhoods could not, even remotely, have afforded to pay the exorbitant fare. Their situation is, to our certain knowledge, frequently even more terrible than yours. We already donate considerable sums to philanthropic organisations devoted to helping victims of violence. You must understand that our resources are limited. We are afraid that we have no alternative but to demand that you go away."

If, for the kind of reasons outlined here, anyone turned away a woman who had been attacked, their behaviour would be strongly disapproved. Most probably they would feel shame. In this society the story of the Good Samaritan still resonates. Once we become aware of an appeal for help from an individual whose suffering we know is real and whom we have the capacity to assist, a human relationship is established. It is within our power to act generously or ungenerously. It is no longer within our power to pretend that in the appeal to us for help nothing of significance has occurred. Whatever we do, for good or for ill, we will have to live with the consequences. Perhaps we could call the fact that certain kinds of obligation arise from the presence of an individual of whose plight they have made us aware the ethics of proximity.

Although the analogies are not perfect, there are important similarities between an individual's obligations to the person in desperate need who appears at their door and a nation's obligations to asylum seekers, fleeing persecution, who arrive at its border. In both cases the ethics of proximity apply. It would, almost self-evidently, be wrong to turn one's back on a woman who had been brutally assaulted because of a belief that there are some in a situation even worse than hers or that if we offered her help others would soon beat a path to our door. Similarly it has been wrong to inform those fleeing from savage persecution, whose cases we have discovered to be genuine, that because those in Third World camps are in an even more desperate situation or because if we treated them generously others would, almost certainly, try to exploit our generosity, we have no alternative but to treat them harshly as a warning to others, or even to turn them away.

The ethics of proximity identify the difference between the kind of obligations we owe to the fourteen million refugees in the world and to the twelve thousand or so who tried to reach Australia between 1999 and 2001. There is little we can do for the overwhelming majority of the fourteen million. There is a great deal we could have done – and can still do – for the twelve thousand who, simply through their arrival in Australia or even their thwarted attempts to get here, established a relationship with Australia and who now fall, through their proximity, within a field of ethical obligation which we cannot avoid. While all this might sound rather abstract, in fact a powerful sense of obligation to these asylum seekers, including even those who have been transported to Nauru, has influenced, often deeply, the lives of the very many Australians who have been dismayed by the brutal way their government has, thus far, treated the fourth-wave asylum seekers from Iraq, Afghanistan and Iran.

Most of the Afghan refugees now in Australia fled from the Taliban. Most of the Iraqi refugees fled from Saddam Hussein. Given that both these regimes have now been overthrown, why should Australians now not repatriate, according to the process established by law, the fourth-wave refugees from Afghanistan and Iraq?

There are two fundamental answers to this question. The first is implicit in what we have already argued. For different reasons, in post-Taliban Afghanistan and in post-Saddam Iraq circumstances are exceptionally insecure and unpredictable and, in general, as each month passes, growing worse.

For many of the Afghan refugees the local political, ethnic or religious conditions that caused them to flee have persisted despite the overthrow of the Taliban and the installation of the Hamid Karzai government, whose authority scarcely extends beyond Kabul. Most of the Afghan refugees in Australia are Hazaras. Many are extremely well-informed about the situation in their districts or villages. Sometimes their fears concern localised Pashtun–Hazara tension; sometimes the remnants of Taliban or al-Qaeda, or other Sunni Muslim fundamentalists; sometimes what they fear is the power of local clerics who do not look kindly on people who have been influenced by secular attitudes in the West; sometimes they are even aware of inter-Hazara conflicts of a ferocious kind. Because of their extraordinary complexity and variety it is virtually impossible for Department of Immigration public servants or Refugee Review Tribunal members to understand the micro-political situations in the towns and villages of contemporary, post-Taliban Afghanistan. Because of these local circumstances many of the Afghan refugees who have been repatriated, mainly from Nauru, have felt too frightened to go home and have fled again, after a short stay in Kabul, to Pakistan or Iran.

The situation in Iraq is different. Under the Anglo–American occupation, daily life, especially for urban Iraqis, has become even more difficult than it was under Saddam. In part there is the problem of continuing low-intensity war – the attacks by insurgents and terrorists and the often indiscriminate or clumsy military response to them by the occupying force. In part there is now a terrible problem of lawlessness – murders, rapes, assaults, armed robberies, carjackings, kidnapping for ransom and so on. And in part there is the problem of economic breakdown – massive unemployment and the unreliability or non-availability of basic services like electricity, gas, water and sewage.

Nor are there grounds for optimism about the future. Iraq is an impoverished country with a recent totalitarian past and no liberal or democratic traditions on which to draw. It is divided between Shia and Sunni Muslims; between Arabs and Kurds; between Islamists and democrats; between a devout populace and a secular middle class. Chaos is inevitable. The chance of civil war is real. Given the extreme perilousness of the present and the unpredictability of the future, repatriation ought not even to be contemplated for a very considerable time. Needless to say, endlessly reviewed temporary protection visas are not a legitimate means of postponing the decision to repatriate until the time seems right.

Yet there is an even more powerful argument against repatriation than this. Let us call this argument "enough is enough".

When Isaac Deutscher wanted to explain the typical experiences of the communists who came to power in Eastern Europe after the Second World War, he wrote the fictitious biography of someone he called a "Polrugarian Minister". For our part, in imitation of Isaac Deutscher, we should like to explain why no Afghan or Iraqi (or Iranian) temporary protection visa holder should be repatriated by inventing a life of our own, of someone we shall call an "Iranistaqi" refugee.

Muhammed is a forty-year-old Sunni Muslim. He comes from a moderately prosperous farming family. As a conscripted teenager he was badly wounded in a savage nine-year war between Iranistaq and a neighbouring power. When the war was over, a cruel Shia-dominated police state was established. In the late 1980s his father and maternal uncle fell under suspicion for dissident activities and were, shortly after, executed. Two of Muhammed's brothers fled to the United States. In the mid-1990s he was arrested and severely tortured before being released. Muhammed's mother sold the family farm and encouraged her son to escape. He left behind with her a wife and a child.

Muhammed fled to a neighbouring country carrying with him the proceeds of the sale. Here he learned of a people smuggler who could arrange a passage to Europe, Canada or Australia. Muhammed could afford only the Australian fare. He was supplied by the smuggler with false papers and took a circuitous route to Indonesia, where he huddled for several weeks in a filthy hotel room, hiding from the local police. Eventually another smuggler established contact. Muhammed was driven by bus to a small Javanese port. With more than three hundred others he was commanded to board a small, unseaworthy fishing boat. During the voyage the weather was bad; Muhammed was convinced they all would die. When, after nine days, the boat reached Christmas Island, he was overjoyed.

Muhammed was taken to a primitive camp called Port Hedland. For ten days a dozen fellow Iranistaqi asylum seekers were held in isolation. Muhammed then told his story to an official. He was informed he had been "screened in". Did this mean, he asked, that he could leave the camp? The official laughed. For very many months Muhammed remained at Port Hedland. Nothing happened. For the first four months he was unable even to telephone his wife. After five months he was provided with a lawyer from Melbourne and interviewed. Several weeks later he was notified that his case had been rejected. He did not understand why. At Port Hedland a number of Iranistaqi asylum seekers, in a position similar to his, in their despair went on hunger strikes. Muhammed joined in.

His lawyer arranged the appeal, and Muhammed's Tribunal case was heard by video-link between Port Hedland and Melbourne. Three months later he discovered that the Tribunal had decided that he was a refugee. He had now been in detention for more than eighteen months. He had been having regular nightmares where the experiences of being wounded in war and interrogated by secret police merged with his detention in strange ways. He knew that he had become seriously ill, as he put it, "in his mind".

Muhammed also knew that, because of his temporary visa, he would never be able to apply for his wife and child to join him. He encouraged her to borrow from a cousin in Germany and leave Iranistaq. In October 2001 he learned that his wife and child had made it to Indonesia. With many others they set out for Ashmore Reef. Their boat was impounded by the Australian Navy. All were taken first to a camp on Christmas Island, and then to Nauru. They were lucky. In September 2002 the Department of Immigration found that Muhammed's wife and child were refugees. The family were reunited in Sydney. Like Muhammed, his wife and child had been granted three-year temporary visas.

Shortly after Muhammed's wife reached Australia, Iranistaq was invaded and the foul regime overthrown as part of the US War on Terror. A letter from the Department of Immigration arrived in mid-2003, which offered $10,000 to the family to return. The family were given six months to decide. Muhammed's visa had by now expired. He believed there would soon be a new hearing of his case. Unofficially he was advised by a Department public servant that he had little chance of success. Because he had not applied for the renewal of his visa before 27 September 2001, it was explained, the best he could hope for anyhow was another temporary one. Muhammed phoned his mother in his village. She begged him not to come home. "Iranistaq is hell." He no longer knew what to do, or for what to hope.

This is an invented but by no means a fanciful or exaggerated tale. There are now thousands of refugees in Australia with experiences similar to Muhammed's and in a situation very close to his. There is, or so it seems to us, only so much a human being can endure. Is it really necessary that all these TPVs should now face another hearing of their protection case, a new round of appeals to the Refugee Review Tribunal, the Federal Court, to the Minister? Is it right that these people should have to choose between a return to detention, or repatriation to a country which once they fled and now they fear? Have these people not already suffered enough? Has the word mercy lost its resonance in Australia?

Since the *Tampa* "crisis", Operation Relex and the adoption of the Pacific Solution, precisely one asylum seeker boat, with fifty-three Vietnamese on board, has managed to reach Australia's shores. These asylum seekers were detained on Christmas Island. It seems likely that they will eventually be repatriated. Later in 2003 a second boat, with fourteen Turkish Kurds on board, reached Melville Island. It was sent back to Indonesia by the Australian Navy. At first the government claimed, implausibly and, as it turned out, falsely, that those on board had not sought asylum. It then claimed that whether or not they had sought asylum was irrelevant. The government had discovered a loophole in the law. As soon as the Kurds reached Melville Island it gazetted a new regulation which excluded Melville Island from Australia's migration zone. As it happens, regulations come into force at midnight of the day they are gazetted. Although the government must have been aware that the new regulations would most likely soon be rejected by the Senate (which had already knocked back a government plan to excise several thousand offshore islands), before that happened it was able to claim that the Kurds had landed on an island outside Australia's migration zone. By replication of this action, no asylum seeker boats landing on Australia's northern coastline need ever be processed again.

Nor is it only the boats which have, since *Tampa*, been effectively deterred. Over the past two and a half years very few "unauthorised arrivals" have reached Australian airports and succeeded in making an asylum claim before being turned around. In the financial year 2002–03 a total of twenty "unauthorised arrivals" at airports were able to make a protection claim. Even the number of asylum claims made by "authorised arrivals" has dropped dramatically in recent times. In parliament on 12 February 2003, the Minister for Immigration boasted about Australia's success in reducing the number of asylum claims by 50 per cent in the previous year, from twelve thousand to six thousand. Almost all of these applications now come from people who arrive on valid student or tourist visas. The success rate of such claims is very low – perhaps one in twenty. As a consequence of all this, in mid-2003 Mr Ruddock was able to announce that a mere seven hundred places had notionally been allocated to successful onshore asylum seekers for the coming year, a reduction from a notional two thousand in the previous year and from a real allocation of 5577 onshore asylum seeker places at the height of the fourth wave of unauthorised arrivals in 2000–01. It is commonly claimed that the Department of Immigration is driven by a "culture of control". The Department has now, to its great satisfaction, regained control over the twelve thousand places of the humanitarian element of Australia's migration program. Australia is, accordingly, more or less an asylum seeker-free zone. In the eyes of Philip Ruddock, Amanda Vanstone and John Howard, we are now the envy of the Western world, for, in the instantly famous words of the Prime Minister during the 2001 election campaign, almost alone among Western nations, "We decide who comes here and the circumstances in which they come."

Concerning the future of asylum seeker policy there are now two central questions to consider, one general and one particular. The general question concerns what is to be done about the increasingly punitive anti-asylum seeker system introduced progressively from the early 1990s, whose most important features are mandatory detention, temporary protection, stiff penalties for people smugglers, naval repulsion at the border and Pacific island processing centres. The particular question concerns what is to happen to the nearly ten thousand people facing possible repatriation – the nine thousand or so on temporary protection visas; and the five hundred or more who are presently either in long-term detention in Australia or on Nauru because their asylum claims have failed but they are too frightened to go home.

Even though the general and the particular issues overlap, these questions need to be considered separately. Even more importantly, the particular question of the ten thousand should be given priority over the general question of the future of asylum seeker policy. The reason can be stated like this. The general question will take considerable time to resolve; the arguments are complex; there are genuinely great difficulties to resolve. By contrast, in considering the particular fate of the almost ten thousand who are presently trapped in the purgatory of temporary protection or in the hell of long-term detention, the issues are simple and a resolution urgent. On this question the well-being of considerable numbers of innocent human beings now depends. Australia's asylum seeker system, as we have tried to show, inflicts very real damage on the norms of civilised international behaviour. On the other hand, precisely because it works as a deterrent system, it does not cause present harm to individual asylum seekers, who look – perhaps vainly – to other countries for their protection needs. Yet precisely because the pre-*Tampa* deterrent system failed to deter, it has left as its legacy ten thousand human beings in detention or threatened with repatriation, whose lives Australia now is in a position either to redeem or, alternatively, to destroy. There are arguments, for and against, a system of asylum seeker deterrence which works. There are no arguments for the continued targetting of people trapped by the logic of an obsolete deterrent system – based on mandatory detention and temporary protection – which failed. Since the institution of an almost entirely effective deterrent system at the border, no possible purpose is served by continuing to punish unsuccessful asylum seekers by keeping them permanently locked up, or by refusing to those whose asylum claims succeeded and who were accepted as genuine refugees the chance of a permanent home and a new life. To maintain mandatory detention and temporary protection of these people in the present circumstances is an exercise either in bureaucratic inertia or in cruelty of an entirely purposeless kind. Nor is any present purpose served by the continued detention in offshore processing centres of those caught in the transition from an ineffective to an effective deterrent system.

What, then, in the short-term, is to be done? All temporary protection visa holders should be granted permanent residence. All those in Australia who have been detained already for far too long should be released at once. This should include not only women and children but also men. All those in Nauru should be brought to Australia. In acknowledgement of the harm already suffered, all long-term detainees should be granted permanent residence. We owe it to these people. The numbers are now small. Finally, whether or not the system of naval deterrence at the border is maintained – and, on balance, we believe that because of the damage it inflicts on the UN Refugee Convention, it should not be – Australia must never again inflict mandatory detention on asylum seekers, temporary protection on refugees, except in cases like the Kosovars, or send anyone to disgraceful processing camps like the ones on Manus

Island and Nauru. It is simply unthinkable that if ever there were to be a fifth wave of asylum seekers fleeing tyrannies who reached Australia, they should be treated in the cold and brutal way the Iraqis, Afghans and Iranians have been treated by Australia since 1999.

SOURCES

1–3   The best study of the arrival of the Vietnamese by boat and its political con-
      sequences is Nancy Viviani, *The Long Journey: Vietnamese Migration and Settlement in
      Australia*, Melbourne University Press, Melbourne, 1984.

2–5   Andrew Hamilton S.J. analysed the story of the Cambodian asylum seekers in
      Eureka Street, 3 (1), February 1993; 3 (2), March 1993 and 4 (3), April 1994.
      For a legal analysis of the early period of mandatory detention see Mary
      Crock, "Climbing Jacob's Ladder: The High Court and the Administrative
      Detention of Asylum Seekers in Australia", *Sydney Law Review*, 15 (338), 1993
      and Mary Crock, "The Evolution of the Law and Policy Governing the
      Detention of Asylum-seekers in Australia", *Migration Monitor*, October 1993.
      Many of the issues involved in the second and third waves are discussed in
      Frank Brennan, *Tampering with Asylum: A Universal Humanitarian Problem*, University
      of Queensland Press, St Lucia, 2003.

5   Here and elsewhere the details of particular boat arrivals have been derived
      from DIMIA Fact Sheet no. 74A http://www.immi.gov.au/facts/
      74a_boatarrivals.htm.

9   William Maley uses the metaphor of the lottery in, for example, Robert
      Manne (ed.), *The Howard Years*, Black Inc., Melbourne, 2003, p. 147. David
      Corlett uses the metaphor of the heap in his doctoral thesis "The Politics of
      Exclusion: Australia and asylum seekers", La Trobe University, 2003.

12–14 The best account of this episode is David Marr & Marian Wilkinson, *Dark
      Victory*, Allen & Unwin, Crows Nest, 2003.

16   The figures for RRT appeals success come from Frank Brennan's *Tampering with
      Asylum*, p. 158. The figures of long-term detainees were given to a hearing of
      the Legal and Constitution Committee of the Senate on 4 November 2003.

17   The number of self-harm incidents comes from *'Damaging Kids'* – Children in
      Department of Immigration and Multicultural and Indigenous Affairs' Immigration Detention
      Centre, CCJFP Occasional Paper no. 12, 3 May 2002.

19–21 The report of the Joint Committee on Foreign Affairs, Defence and Trade can
      be found at http://www.aph.gov.au/house/committee/jfadt.

21–2 Sev Ozdowski, *A Report on Visits to Immigration Detention Facilities by the Human
      Rights Commissioner 2001* is found at http://www.humanrights.gov.au/
      human_rights/idc/index.html.

22–3 Louis Joinet's report of the Working Group on Arbitrary Detention can be
      found at http://www.unhcr.ch/Huridocda/Huridocda.nsf/0/6035497b
      015966fec1256cc200551f19/ $FILE/G0215391.pdf.

23 Aamer Sultan & Kevin O'Sullivan, "Psychological disturbances in asylum seekers held in long-term detention: a participant-observer account", *Medical Journal of Australia*, no. 175, 2001, pp. 593–96.

23–4 Zachary Steel, "The Politics of Exclusion and Denial: The Mental Health Costs of Australia's Refugee Policy", paper to 38th Congress Royal Australian and New Zealand College of Psychiatrists, Hobart, 12–15 May 2003.

24–9 For the story of Shayan Badraie see Human Rights and Equal Opportunity Commission Report of an Inquiry into a complaint by Mr Mohammed Badraie on behalf of his son Shayan regarding acts or practices of the Commonwealth of Australia (the Department of Immigration and Multi-cultural and Indigenous Affairs) at http://www.hreoc.gov.au/human_rights/human_rights_reports/hrc_25.html.
The family's case for protection was reviewed by the Refugee Review Tribunal, Tribunal Member: Paula Cristoffanini, 7 August 2002, Sydney. See also Karen J. Zwi, Brenda Herzberg, David Dosseter and Jyotsna Field, "A child in detention: dilemmas faced by health professionals", *Medical Journal of Australia*, 179, 15 September 2003, pp. 319–322 and ABC, Four Corners, *The Inside Story*, 13 August 2001, http://www.abc.net.au/4corners/stories/s344246.htm.
The interview with Mohammed Badraie was in Sydney on 30 October 2003.

31 The quotation from Philip Ruddock can be found in Michael Leach & Fethi Mansouri, *Critical Perspectives on Refugee Policy in Australia*, Deakin University, Burwood, 2003, p. 103.

33 There are a number of studies of TPV holders, R. Mann, *Temporary Protection Holders in Queensland*, Queensland Government, Brisbane, 2001; F. Mansouri and M. Bagdas, *Politics of Social Exclusion: Refugees on Temporary Protection Visas in Victoria*, Deakin University, Burwood, 2002; Paul Foley, *The Impact of the Commonwealth's Temporary Protection Visa Policy in South Australia*, SA Government, Adelaide, 2003; Greg Marston, *Temporary Protection, Permanent Uncertainty: The experience of refugees living on temporary protection visas*, Centre for Applied Social Research, RMIT University, 2003.

34 Mary Crock & Ben Saul, *Future Seekers: Refugees and the Law in Australia*, The Federation Press, Leichardt, 2002.

34–7 Interview with Ahmed Alzalimi in Sydney on 29 October 1999. See also David Marr & Marian Wilkinson, *Dark Victory*, ch. 18.

39–40 The quotation from Paula Fernandes and the study come from Zachary Steel's "The Politics of Exclusion and Denial ..."

40–2 A copy of a translation of "Dr" Habib's taped suicide message is in our possession. There is some dispute about whether the translation is entirely accurate. A number of the Hazara community of Murray Bridge, South Australia have been interviewed as has Habib's father in Kabul (by telephone) on 19 November 2003.

43–6   On the politics of the Pacific Solution see David Marr & Marian Wilkinson, *Dark Victory*, esp. ch. 8. Also very useful is the Senate, *Select Committee on a Certain Maritime Incident*, Commonwealth of Australia, Canberra, 2002, chs. 10 and 11.

47–51   The material on which this section is mainly based are the letters and emails from Topside camp at Nauru made available to us by Elaine Smith. Occasionally the spelling, grammar or an obviously wrong word have been corrected for ease of comprehension.

51–4   Dr Maarten Dormaar's IOM reports and his resignation speech circulated freely by email in 2002–03.

55–8   We have relied on the daily press, Elaine Smith's emails and Senator Vanstone's media releases.

61–2   The quotation from Kofi Annan can be found in Press Release SG/SM/8894 AFG/230, 24 September 2003.
       The closure of UNHCR offices was announced in UNHCR Information Update 1, Issue 47, 15 December 2003, Kabul.

62   Andrew Wilkie's comments were made on ABC television's *Lateline* program on 17 February 2004. See http://www.abc.net.au/lateline/content/ 2004/s1047307.htm.

63–5   The story of Mohammad Mussa Nazari is based on interviews conducted on 14 December 2003 with a group of Malistan Afghans and with Mussa's brother by telephone on the same day.

65   The story of Hassan is based on an interview with Marion Le and a telephone conversation with Hassan in Quetta, Pakistan on 7 January 2004. Here and elsewhere in this section the true names of returnees have not been used.

67   Julie Macken in the *Australian Financial Review*, 2 May 2003, p. 88. Ruddock's comment is in House Hansard, 28 May 2003, p. 15, 336. Joinet's comments were broadcast on ABC Radio National, *Background Briefing*, 8 June 2003.

68   Minute, File No. PCF2002/454, Central Office.

71–2   The source of this story has spoken to Jamal regularly by telephone since his return.

72   Russell Skelton's reports appeared in the *Age* on 16 and 17 February 2004.

73–4   Hussein's story is based on interviews with two people who knew him. They took place on 23 July 2003 and 29 October 2003.

74–5   Regular contact has been maintained with the Kadem family both in Australia and Iraq.

75   We know of three other Iraqi returnees who, like the Kadems, were sent by the International Organisation of Migration across the Jordanian border to Iraq at night. One man was forced to pay hundreds of dollars in bribes to the Iraqi police who questioned his Australian papers.

75   The Edmund Rice Centre has conducted research into the plight of returnees from Australia. It found that Australian officials had encouraged detainees, including Iraqis, to use false passports to leave Australia. The Australian immigration department also issued detainees with tickets to places they did not have visas to enter and encouraged them to bribe overseas immigration officials. The ERC's interim report, "No Liability – Tragic Results from Australia's Deportations" is online at http://www.erc.org.au/research/pdf/1071789275.pdf.

76–7   Information on the current state of primary and RRT decisions regarding further protection visas was supplied by the Department of Immigration and Multicultural and Indigenous Affairs, 18 February 2004. Additional information was presented to the Senate Legal and Constitutional Legislation Committee, 17 February 2004.

79, 81–2 An analogy between the asylum seekers and a woman to whom violence has been done was discussed in David Corlett's doctoral thesis. Here the idea is taken in a slightly different direction.

85   Isaac Deutscher's essay, "The Tragic Life of a Polrugarian Minister" is in his *Heretics and Renegades: and other essays*, Cape, London, 1969.

87   One also reached an excised territory, Cocos Island.

Phillip Knightley

Yes, David, there will always be the bond of a shared language and a cultural heritage between Australia and Britain. And, yes, the way the Mother Country tumbled us out of the nest was the making of us. I just wish she could have been a little more motherly and gracious about it, a little less selfish, cold and pragmatic.

Take that pommy bastard Sir Otto Niemeyer, a director of the Bank of England. He came to Australia in 1930 to tell us how to manage our financial affairs. He decided that the trouble was the Australian character and the Australian way of life. Australians had a natural optimism and this was very, very bad. Ordinary Australians had to be stripped of their belief that something would always turn up. And our living standards were too high, so wages had to be cut and cut again.

When he said this at a civic reception in Adelaide, the very same paper that reported his remarks, the *Evening News*, carried an item about Depression children starving, actually starving, in the Granville electorate.

Historians' arguments about the fall of Singapore and the Anglo–American plan to concentrate on the war in Europe before turning to Japan – even if it meant temporarily leaving Australia to the Japanese – have rumbled on for so long as to risk becoming boring. But was it too much to ask of Mother that if she was planning to abandon us to save herself she might at least have told us?

No wonder Curtin said that from then on we were going to look to the United States as our protector. Although if Australia imagines that its loyalty to Uncle Sam in the recent war against Iraq now guarantees that the USA will always be there for us, a glance at any of the Washington plans setting out American geographical strategic interests for the twenty-first century will come as a bit of a shock. Where does Australia figure in them? Nowhere.

All right, Britain's decision to end its traditional Empire trade arrangements and join the European Common Market was a shock but turned out to be good for us in the economic long run. But how can we forgive Mother for the 1971

Immigration Act, a nasty piece of legislation that many found the most painful betrayal of all? At a stroke it ended the right Australians had enjoyed since the founding of the country in 1788 to free entry into Britain and full equality with their kith and kin. A former editor of the London *Telegraph*, William Deedes, commented, "We should acknowledge that for our growing estrangement from Australia we carry most of the blame."

So, Mother, let's agree that we will still talk to each other because we share the same language and memories, but we have left home for good and will not be back. We are not a republic yet, but one day we will be and in the meantime we're a country very different from you and the Old World.

This was brought home to me at the Australia Day celebrations at Australia House in London – an evening of hiccups, happiness and mini meat pies. It ended with a stirring "Advance Australia Fair", in tune, in time and everyone knew the words. Later, walking down a freezing Strand it occurred to me that as a national anthem, "Advance Australia Fair" has got it about right. I cannot support the sentiments expressed in "*aux armes citoyens*", or in "the rockets' red glare", and certainly not in saving of an elderly English lady whose only danger is probably from her daughter's dogs. But I can wholeheartedly support the advancement of an independent young nation which offers wealth for toil. And that about sums it up.

Phillip Knightley

Morag Fraser

One of the odder, happier antiphons of this past summer was David Malouf's essay and its rippling, comic echo in the cricket commentary of Harsha Bogle and Kerry O'Keeffe. In the intervals between play you could read the one in all its reasoned complexity, and then, with the batsmen back at the crease, listen to the anarchic balancing of the other, and marvel at an accident of collaboration.

The conceit of the inspired pairing of the Indian Bogle and the Australian O'Keeffe was that they would not understand one another. Different cultures, different styles, the Subcontinental gentleman set up by the larrikin leg break bowler. But of course both knew exactly how to play the game, and the "chemistry" that made them such good listening, in part personal flair, was in equal part a shared, complex, colonial and post-colonial history. Their common ground – for all the linguistic sledging – was language, and the common bond, reason – the English (or Scottish) Enlightenment rationality which Malouf convincingly argues is our distinguishing inheritance.

And what hay they made with it! O'Keeffe, in Falstaffian mode, would test the civilised, rational limits, and Bogle would play along in mock (or sometimes genuine?) shock. But both kept the commentary flowing. Both understood the rules, written and tacit. They also understood how much lethal passion is displaced in play, and what cathartic fun is to be had in experimenting, in mucking around, in playing games. Word games, food games – lamingtons for tea – cricket games. "It is small things that make up the real fabric of a relationship;" writes Malouf, "things that 'history' may not know about or miss. But then sport is just the sort of area where to make too much of a good thing would be to miss the real thing altogether."

Exactly. It is that lightness about being Australian that Malouf's essay so profoundly catches, and expresses – a condition of lightness that acknowledges the experiential rather than the essential nature of who we are. "It keeps us on our toes, as curious observers of ourselves," Malouf writes. Indeed, it does. And how flat-footed it makes most of our entrenched conflicts seem, how leaden and unimaginative our dualisms, current or historical. White Australia/coloured Australia; new Australian/old Australian; black armband history/white armband history. If only we would learn to live with richness, with complexity, instead of trying, for motives malign, political or simply anxious, to tie everything down, ourselves included. If only this, or Malouf's Boyer lectures that preceded it, could have been the preamble to the reductive republican debate we had, and the equally polarised ones – about the republic, about race relations, about international alliances – we seem doomed to have in future. If only our press, electronic media and politics would take a few minutes to go into the detail that dignifies most human intercourse.

Then we could debate in a fruitful way the current transformation of some of the institutions that Malouf adduces as the underpinning of Australia's exceptional peace and prosperity. We could look at the Westminster tradition of a disinterested, committed public service that he lauds and ask if we still have it. We could examine our strategic alliances in the light of the complicated history he explores, without banal, reflex accusations of anti-Americanism. We could debate our place in the Asia-Pacific region without prejudice or lies. We could take up words like "reconciliation" again without tasting ash in our mouths.

We might look further, and profitably, at the Scottish as well as the Irish inheritance in Australia (as does Don Watson in *Caledonia Australis*, or Les Murray in his 1980 essay "The Bonnie Disproportion"). We might think about the Scots' almost obsessive emphasis on education – for all the people – and ask whether, like Robert Menzies, we still share that obsession. We might even talk more about language and its long reach. We might ponder the lightness of the complex, ironic poetry of Geoffrey Chaucer who, even before Shakespeare, so anchored his verse and his quicksilver, searching mind in the concrete stuff of everyday life that he turned around a French occupation and gave his people back a language large enough to answer to their most extravagant imaginings.

Essays have a much longer shelf life than daily news. So perhaps we shall do all these things. It can't hurt to hope.

Morag Fraser

Larissa Behrendt

David Malouf's evocative account of the Australia of his childhood is a personal narrative of what it means to be Australian. There is an intimacy in his nostalgia for the Australia of his youth – one in which we can see Rita Hayworth on the big screen, hear Bing Crosby singing "White Christmas" and taste the bread-and-butter pudding. *Made in England* proudly acknowledges a British inheritance whose culture and values are so adopted into everyday life here in the antipodes that we hardly noticed that they were not ours. This easy integration is, as Malouf acknowledges, both a testament to the diversity of "British" culture and the diversity of "Australian" experience.

This is a different perspective on Australia to the one evoked by Germaine Greer in her essay *Whitefella Jump Up*. Malouf sees the normality of our British idiosyncrasies in his childhood where adaptation is as natural as ownership; Greer sees a discomfort and a cringe in the inability of white Australians to find their place here. Hers is a country where the sense of belonging needs to be cultivated and a feeling of acceptance needs to be learnt.

Both Malouf and Greer understand that it is only through the past that the way forward can be grasped. For Malouf, the acknowledgement of all that is solid and reliable about the cornerstones of our inherited British system of laws and governance provides the necessary confidence to look towards a content and independent Australia. Ours is a country blessed with a history of peaceful political change and the stability of the rule of law. For Greer, confessions of the inability to embrace Aboriginal experience and the treatment of Aboriginal people are the keys to an imagined future Australia where non-Indigenous people feel as at ease with this country as the original custodians.

In these assessments of what Australia was, is and may become, it is hard to forget Don Watson's pessimistic and fatalistic essay, *Rabbit Syndrome*. As someone who was present when Paul Keating delivered the Redfern Park speech, I found much that resonated in Watson's lament for the changing course of Australia.

As an Aboriginal person, I see the turn away from the acknowledgement of Indigenous presence and culture as alienating. As Malouf writes: we find it so difficult to imagine any history but the one we have actually experienced. Malouf, as much as Greer, sees the acknowledgement of Indigenous presence and experience as a central part of an honest Australian persona.

Malouf's contribution to this debate is that he acknowledges that, without the seeds of where we come from we would not be where we are now and, more importantly, would not have the same ability to determine our future. He makes a powerful argument that there is much to celebrate in that history which the recognition of historical truths that are unpalatable and shameful could not erase. I've never understood the argument that acknowledging the mistreatment of Indigenous people and saying "sorry" was a way of making Australians feel ashamed of their past. Recognition and acceptance of the past – even those things that we wished we had done differently – does not mean that we somehow lose the ability to appreciate all that there is to be proud about. Either view – all positive or all doom-and-gloom – is too superficial to be helpful in creating character and shaping identity.

Identity is as much defined by the way you see yourself as it is created by the way that others see you. Our idea of who we are is not just formed through our internal distinctiveness but also through our experience with others and the stereotypes society lays before us. It is shaped by self-expression and through our interaction with others, our socialisation by family, education and community, and our positive and negative experience in the world. Who we are is a process, transformed by our intellectual, emotional and spiritual growth, moulded by the actions, judgements and expectations of others. Our identity has a narcissistic, introverted and existential aspect that has the need for space and freedom for self-expression. It also has a symbiotic communal, extroverted and fraternal aspect that requires public space and institutional arrangements that provide the space and freedom to do as we wish.

The strength of Malouf's essay lies in his ability to connect the trappings of culture and language to their institutional form. The relationship between society and its institutions is one that is often overlooked or downplayed. Laws are only a reflection of the society that makes them. Perhaps the best, and most quoted, example of this phenomenon is that Stalin's Russia had a Bill of Rights. Our laws mean nothing if they are not enacted into a society that has the political, social and ethical will to ensure that they are interpreted and applied in the way they are intended to be.

However, there is one trap in the exaltation of our current legal system.

We can all acknowledge that the common law is the most superior form of legal system and that the Westminster system the most democratic form of government, but that should not lead to the conclusion that they are perfect. Nor can the nobility of their principle lead to the supposition that they are implemented in the spirit in which they were intended. In fact, for all of the cornerstones of British law that we inherit – innocent until proven guilty, the rule of law, separation of powers, free elections – there are many examples of the way in which the gaps in that common law have led to the gross violation of human rights, particularly of the poor, marginalised, culturally distinct.

Malouf's example of slavery raises this very issue. It is often held to be a distinguishing feature of the superiority of our legal system that there has never been an institutionalised form of slavery as part of our laws and that, as a result, we have avoided the hypocrisy of creating social and moral stigma while espousing egalitarianism. That may be the case that can be argued when looking at the black and white of the statute books. But Pacific Islanders who were "blackbirded" and Aboriginal people who were unpaid for their work on cattle stations and in the kitchens of middle-class Australia found little comfort in the lack of legal sanction for the deprivation of their liberty and the exploitation of their labour. The fact that we have a system of laws that is silent on rights protection and therefore allows such violations of commonly assumed liberties without the need for formal laws is one of the more unfortunate legacies of our constitutional heritage. Idolisation of the English system of government often leads to the "if it ain't broke, don't fix it" attitude that sees endorsement of laws if they work for the rich, middle-class and culturally dominant rather than measuring them against the way they work for the poor, marginalised and culturally distinct.

Malouf's honest affection and insightful reflections on Australia and its embrace of British culture, like all powerful ideas, will be misinterpreted and exploited by those who are engaged in Australia's vicious "culture wars". Those who have sought to discredit the "black armband" view of Australia understand better than anyone how the values of society shape our institutions. These fierce debates focus on the telling of history, the squabbling about numbers killed on the frontier and the debates over the proper legal definition of "genocide". But they are not discussions about "Aboriginal history"; the experience and perspectives of Indigenous people remains unchanged by semantic and numerical debates by academics. They are, instead, a battle about "non-Aboriginal" history and, more importantly, "white" identity. It is a debate whose results will have a profound influence on the values of our society for years to come and will determine whether we move towards tolerance, acceptance, co-existence and diversity, or whether we continue to move towards intolerance, suspicion, fear and conformity. It is because the stakes are so high that this war has been waged through so many of our cultural institutions, including the Australian Broadcasting Commission and the National Museum of Australia.

The use of Malouf's essay to merely extol the virtues of our British past would misrepresent the undercurrent of recognition of Indigenous experience beneath his honest affection for what it is that makes us proud to be Australian. The real promise of his essay is that, if we are as truthful about what makes us great as we are about what we could have done better, we will be better equipped, more confident, as a nation to choose a dynamic, independent, unique and exciting future. I think Greer, and even Watson, would agree with that proposition even if their blueprints for that pathway would be vastly different.

Aboriginal Australia has long embraced its diversity while struggling to maintain a unified national front. We will continue to watch with interest as our fellow Australians struggle with their own identity crisis.

Larissa Behrendt

Alan Atkinson

It goes without saying that David Malouf's essay, *Made in England*, is a wonderfully subtle and authoritative knitting together of past events and present concerns. But there seems to be something missing in the heart of what he has to say. It is strange to find in such a lengthy discussion of the impact of empire on Australia, or more precisely of "Australia's British inheritance", such a cheerfully unproblematic account of the uses of power. Anyone who has taken any notice of the current History Wars must be aware that imperial power, as a force for both good and evil, is a mightily vexed issue among Australians. In Malouf's essay it doesn't sound vexed at all.

The History Wars, toxic and superficial as they have often been, highlight the moral complexity of the Australian past. If we can move beyond caricatures of Britishness and empire – and Malouf has done a great deal to that end – surely Anglo-Australian history looks like a substantial tragedy. Not all evil, of course. The "perpetual lightness", as Malouf calls it, which is now part of Australians' ideal vision of Australia, owes a good deal to the British inheritance. But surely the richness of our national history comes from the way in which that glory, all "sunshiny and warm", can (or ought to) live in the collective mind alongside imagery of chilling darkness. Surely this is the best thing about the British inheritance – the invigorating puzzle it has always offered to the moral imagination of Australians.

Malouf's account seems to side-step such complexity. In his references to first settlement in 1788 he relies very much on the work of Alan Frost. Frost has been responsible over many years for some remarkable scholarly discoveries and insights. But it seems to me that his arguments about the first impact of the British on Australia tend to short-circuit moral issues. His main concern is to argue for foresight and efficiency in the extension of empire. This is the thrust of his well-known argument about Whitehall's reasons for the choice of Botany Bay as a place of penal settlement. Malouf echoes Frost when he says, "Sydney was first and foremost to be a port". In fact this is very doubtful. In order to prove it we would need to explain why Governor Phillip was told to prevent "by every possible means" any contact with British commercial bases in India, China and the islands of the Pacific. Nor was Phillip given any resources for the creation of a port. For some years there was not even a harbour master at Sydney Cove, or a register of shipping.

This old debate is not just a playground for scholars. It has deep significance for our understanding of the long-term trajectory of Australian history from 1788 on. Scholarly hypotheses are nourished by intellectual temperament. The theory that Botany Bay was meant from the beginning to be efficiently linked to the rest of the world is one which grows from a certain type of national story – from a faith in the overriding historical importance of human energy, intellect, enterprise and broad horizons. It is designed to give us a sense that efficiency is in our genes. By these lights, the doers in our history are the ones that matter most.

The other side of the debate moves along quite different tracks. It says that to begin with, in the minds of the founders, settlement was meant to be perfectly isolated. The main advantage of Botany Bay was its distance from everywhere else, making it impossible for convicts to escape. Scholars argue thus, not only because their conclusions seem to be supported by the scanty evidence still surviving but also, once again, because of intellectual temperament. They like to tell their own kind of story, with distinctive themes from beginning to end. The idea of isolation is peculiarly intriguing. They like to forget about the rest of the world and to focus on a nicely bounded place. They are led as a result to wonder about the internal dynamics of the early settlement, the uses of power and the intricate moral underpinning of community. I am overstating the neatness of this two-way scholarly distinction. But it does exist.

The dichotomy works not only for historians. It existed among the settlers themselves. Maybe it has existed among Australians ever since. In an age of economic rationalism it may be hard to admit the enormous intellectual and moral challenge provided by the second possibility. But by pursuing that challenge we can better understand how convict management, and public order as a whole, evolved in the very sophisticated way it did. Failing to admit it, we make much too light of the moral issues confronting the settlers, the tangle of problems arising from the fact that they came here to form a society of criminals within a land of savages.

For present purposes I am not concerned at all with anyone's basic moral temperament, and certainly not David Malouf's. I am concerned with the inner dynamic, the intellectual and moral slant, of a single piece of writing. Writing has its own momentum, a point which applies not only to works of fiction but also to arguments about the past. Begin in a certain way and habits of artistic consistency carry you thereafter in a certain direction.

In this essay the shape of Malouf's beginning leads him, as it seems to me, not so much to ignore as to simplify moral issues. In the same spirit he enters into another, more recent and more anguished historiographical controversy when he says that, "Our history here has been, by most standards, unviolent". His implication must be that national histories can be categorised as either "violent" or "unviolent". The box in which we place them depends on the standard chosen. But surely there are better ways of understanding violence as a national phenomenon. Malouf attributes Australia's "unviolence" (my word) to the lack of any close relationship between armies and government and also to the lack of lawful slavery in our past. In other words he looks for the roots of violence in great national institutions whose violence might have been justified by law. But violence is an aspect of human behaviour, like many others, which can be both formal and informal. It is just like language in that respect – and Malouf's own account of the influence of English goes wonderfully beyond the impact of institutions.

Writing thus about violence Malouf passes over what is surely one of the central glories of Australia's British inheritance. We know that Australian democracy, as it was established in the 1850s, had its ideological roots in Britain. John Hirst has set out some fine detail on that score in his book *The Strange Birth of Colonial Democracy*. We also know that in Australia monarchical institutions and upper houses, similarly British, were meant as a check on democracy. Of course that check was meant partly to protect the interests of property. But, together with the courts of law, it was also meant to protect the workings of conscience and civility. After all, democracy to begin with went easily hand in hand with bigotry, ignorance and (as with anti-Chinese riots) violence.

Questions about violence in Australian history are to be answered not so much by choosing standards as by choosing where to look. Violence and "unviolence" both belong, at least partly, to Australia's British inheritance. Violence was inherent in invasion and conquest. It was perpetuated from place to place partly by the high numbers of men compared with women and children. "Unviolence" must surely have been due to the way British methods of order offered room – just enough, occasionally – for the workings of individual conscience. Thus when "scientific racism" came to Australia in the 1850s it came mainly from the United States. It offered abstract theory and general "truths" about humanity as a counterweight to the promptings of individual conscience. When, on the Victorian goldfields, white Americans mistreated black Americans (forcing them off the footpath for instance), their behaviour was condemned as "un-British". It was inconsistent with the peaceful government of a multi-racial empire.

A French inheritance might have given Australia a powerful sense of intellectual absolutism and of intellectual liberty. A British inheritance seems to have set up a story about the authority and the rights of conscience, the conscience of the state and the conscience of the individual, altogether a strange combination of moral fumbling and fanfare. It's an interesting gift.

Alan Atkinson

James Curran

David Malouf's essay on Australia's British inheritance is a timely reaffirmation of the defining influence of Britishness in Australian national life and culture. Believing that Australians have for too long undervalued their British heritage, Malouf reminds Australians of its enduring legacy to the nation. In the process he gives short shrift to a radical nationalist version of Australian history which, in its eagerness to pin down the precise moment of Australian independence, often portrays the Anglo–Australian relationship as one of mutual antagonism, or, more simplistically, depicts Australia as an impatient child forever pulling at the apron-strings of the "mother country". The so-called "great betrayal" at Singapore in 1942 may continue to provoke the occasional rage – Paul Keating's parliamentary outburst in February 1992 springs to mind – but, as Malouf notes, Australia's attachment to Britain lingered long into the post-war era.

Likewise, in pointing to the desire of all the British dominions to achieve the cherished status of "equality within the Empire", and in emphasising that Federation in 1901 was not powered by a distinctive Australian cultural nationalism railing against a stultifying Britishness, Malouf has thankfully dispensed with the "thwarted nationalism" thesis. In this view Britain – or bourgeois Australian Anglophiles such as R.G. Menzies – has continually conspired to stifle attempts by "true", working-class Australians to realise their national "independence". On occasion, Australians might well have thrown the odd tantrum and taken great delight in kicking the Empire in the shins, but such moments were inevitably followed by fulsome protestations of the nation's loyalty to Britain.

The great strength of Malouf's essay, though, is that he is unafraid to speak in glowing terms about the British inheritance. Unlike many other Australian intellectuals, who would rather subsume the British heritage into the rich tapestry of cultures that now makes up Australian society, Malouf rejoices in the richness of that British past and its manifestation in Australian language and lore, food and song. Moreover he illustrates the ways in which Australians have modified this heritage to suit their own circumstances and how the transplanting of a British culture here differed in quite fundamental ways from the American experience.

Yet there is a curious omission in his treatment of this important topic: race. Malouf hints at the significance of White Australia's demise, but he is reluctant to delve too deeply. He is rightly troubled by the growing tendency to downplay or trivialise the British heritage, but it is precisely because Britishness was so intimately bound up with ideas of "race" that some have been so quick to consign this heritage to the cellar of the Australian consciousness. If we are now a nation of immigrants, so this theory runs, why should the British be afforded pride of place?

The myth of British race patriotism prescribed that Australians were part of an "organic" worldwide community of British peoples. Australians saw in the White Australia policy the means by which their racial homogeneity could be preserved, thereby keeping the ever-present threat of Asia at bay. As historian W.K. Hancock put it in 1930, among Australians "pride of race counted for more than love of country" and, "Defining themselves as 'independent Australian Britons', they believed each word essential and exact, but laid most stress upon the last." White Australia, Hancock argued, was the "indispensable condition of every other Australian policy". When Labor prime ministers Curtin and Chifley defined Australia as a bastion of the "British-speaking race" in the antipodes, it was no clumsy rhetorical stumble (my emphasis). They were giving voice to the fact that Australians essentially saw themselves as a British people who had welded the various English, Irish, Scots and Welsh components of their heritage into an indissoluble whole – such that they were actually more British than the British. It might be troublesome for some to accept, but during the high point of the nationalist era, that is from the late nineteenth century through to the 1960s, Australia's national myth was a British race myth. (Britain, for its part, may well have been multi-racial by the 1950s, but the British themselves never saw fit to enshrine multiculturalism as a national ideal.)

When this intense British race patriotism collapsed around the time of Britain's first, ultimately failed attempt to enter the EEC between 1961 and 1963 (see Stuart Ward's *Australia and the British Embrace: The Demise of the Imperial Ideal*, MUP, 2001) and its decision to withdraw a military presence from East of Suez, Australian political leaders and intellectuals were left somewhat confused as to how to define the nation. Australians did not immediately claim a new identity; they were actually shocked, and in some cases aggrieved, that their British identity had been taken from them. It was nothing less than a crisis of national meaning. As historian Geoffrey Serle, himself an occasional proponent of the radical national school, observed in 1967, "there has been such a decline since the decline of standard imperial rhetoric, that it is difficult to make any sure statement."

The void in national self-definition raised a key question as to the legacy of the British heritage: had it "thwarted" the move to independent nationhood and was it simply an anachronism in a post-nationalist society, or was it the bequest of a genial political culture in which the classic liberal ideas of freedom and tolerance had fostered an environment in which diversity could flourish?

Malouf's essay is both a reflection of this ongoing identity crisis and an answer to it. In accepting and affirming the British heritage he has done much to highlight it as an ongoing source of vitality and vigour in national life (and thereby offered a warning to those who will craft future republican movements).

There now appear to be two differing responses to the problem of "race" and how it is understood in Australian political culture. On the one hand, left-leaning journalists and commentators are quick to tag as "racist" those who do not conform to their own idea and language of tolerance. So rather than treat Pauline Hanson as a reincarnation of 1950s-style assimilationism and the voice of an older Australia which felt betrayed by multiculturalism and globalisation, they cast her instead as a dangerous and malicious throwback to the worst aspects of the days of White Australia. Likewise the Prime Minister, in responding to the appearance of the *Tampa* on the nation's northern coastline, was supposedly seeking to reconstruct the "great white walls" of the White Australia policy. (This despite Howard actually having lifted the official migrant intake during his term in office.) In both cases the "race" card has been played by the media, not by the political protagonists, and in each case it was played without due deference to the lessons which can be drawn from historical experience.

On the other hand, those who cherish the British constitutional and parliamentary heritage but who are embarrassed by the legacy of White Australia and the intensity of Australia's attachment to the British race myth, argue instead that there was a seamless, painless link between the era when Australians saw themselves as "wholly British" and the moment the nation became multicultural. That a nation of Britishers was magically transformed into a "nation of immigrants" from every country and culture, and that the nation was in essence multicultural from the beginning.

The change in how Australians defined themselves was indeed relatively rapid, but that does not obviate the need to explore the reasons for the demise of Britishness nor should it entail ignoring the complexity of its legacy. Some are in fact finding new ways to come to terms with multiculturalism. The Minister for Health, Tony Abbott, once a critic of multiculturalism on the grounds that it detracted from national unity, has recently admitted that he now accepts it as a legitimate idea for the nation. The reason for this dramatic U-turn? He has met some migrants – with no ethnic links to Britain – who supported the monarchy at the 1999 republican referendum. Abbott's "very conservative multiculturalism" in fact envisages a nation of what might be termed multicultural monarchists.

Malouf's contention that imperial sentiment "is not what really moved" the likes of prime ministers Alfred Deakin and George Reid when they spoke to and defined their people, that they were "canny" in using the language of Britishness to secure a place in a powerful empire, similarly stems from an unwillingness to accept the power of the British race myth. On this reading, Deakin and Reid were not being true to themselves and were in fact manipulating a shallow and submissive populace. Such a view misreads the subtle relationship between sentiment and self-interest in Anglo–Australian relations. Australians may well have been fervent in their identification with the British race myth, but this did not cause them to lose sight of their own interests. Menzies' decision to hold off sending Australian troops to the European theatre immediately following the outbreak of the Second World War – before he had received assurances from the British that they would send the fleet in the event of an attack on Australia – is a potent example of the way in which Australian leaders, though "British to their boot-heels", nevertheless were careful to preserve distinctively Australian interests which arose out of the nation's particular geopolitical circumstances.

If Malouf is searching for a way to deal with the problem of race, he could do far worse than turn to W.K. Hancock's notion of Australians being "british – with a small b": that is, a Britishness motivated neither by a belief in the superiority of the British race nor by thoughts of British glory or imperial grandeur, but by the vision of a diverse family comprising many kindreds and languages. Hancock and other liberal intellectuals of his generation had formed the view that Australia's membership of the British Commonwealth actually guarded against the expression of a jingoistic nationalism, that this sense of loyalty to a wider community was a precious gift in a "sundered world of snarling nationalisms". This allowed intellectuals like Hancock to reconcile their Britishness with their liberalism. Malouf is similarly aware that the British inheritance has had a moderating influence on Australian life, and his essay delivers another healthy blow to the radical nationalists, but in skirting gingerly around the problem of race he misses what for many defined their sense of membership of the wider British world – the "crimson thread of kinship".

James Curran

Sara Wills

"Made in England" is not an obvious stamp on my consciousness. Turn my hands over and you may find forms of Englishness etched into palms that still nurture the memory of a motherland. But I do like to think that if I was made in England, in the last twenty years I have been to some extent un-made in Australia. This is not a bad thing. Not bad in the sense that I do not cherish the memory of "boils and chilblains and whitlows"; and not bad in the sense that I have made an effort to disentangle my personal history from the "dense intermingling of cultural associations" that Malouf argues once grounded many Australians "deeply in both place and time, to at least two countries". This un-making in Australia has not involved a disowning or disavowal of my inheritance, but a reckoning with its "quiet defiance".

This is a phrase Peter Craven uses in his introduction to *Made in England*, and it is certainly a quality I admire in Malouf's essay. Malouf's eloquent and intimate recreation of lived Anglo-Australian experience reminds me of the hollowness of much left-liberal (Anglo-) Australian nationalism. As a social historian, I know there are many who would warm to his evocation of the "style" of "a time of pinched horizons", even though it was "a poorer age". Over the last three years, I have interviewed many British migrants who know and to some extent inhabit this "old world translated". Living in the outer suburbs of Melbourne, these are largely people who left difficult lives in Britain, and quietly adapted to suburban life in Australia. Remembering their inheritance is a pleasurable and often deeply moving experience for many who also recognise their new home as a place that has provided increased opportunities. Malouf's essay would be read by many with a feeling described by the writer Cynthia Pretty: "a longing, vague and undefined, that floats through you, leaving behind both a touch of melancholy and an embracing warmth".

I think these kinds of responses are important to acknowledge in order to draw attention to the experience of inheritance as "embodied": that it is a lived and often living experience. Where acknowledged, this is the aspect of Malouf's essay I welcome most. Even though the effect of his early focus on "style" is to emphasise the taste left by an era of "Milk of Magnesia" and "Castor Oil", much of what he argues is true for those who through birth were "made in England". For some of us, certainly, "when we look at the British we see both what we were to begin with and what we have turned out not to be". And appropriately, given that there are over one million British-born residing in Australia, and that Britain remains a major source of our immigrants — 12,510 arrived here from Britain as permanent migrants in the year to June 2003 (topping New Zealand as the main source of Australia's migrants for the first time in eight years) — Malouf acknowledges the new "styles" that emerge from the changing nature of this inheritance: that the story of having been "made in England" is a complex and continuing one. He argues, for example, that Britain was a land where nobody was "native", and that its identity was shaped by "social and emotional ties between individuals based on shared experiences": that it is an identity that has been "experiential rather than essentialist". He notes also that Britishness in Britain "is in fact a multiple phenomenon and one that is continually shifting shape"; and that Australian Britishness is "a very different thing" and "much more difficult to track down and confront". In some respects, therefore, Malouf describes wonderfully the identity tensions produced because Australia was founded by "two small, damp, divided islands". Such relational complexities are implicit in much of what Malouf writes.

More explicit, however, should be the speaking position of this essay, because Malouf's claims prompt me to ask: for whom is it true that the notion of identity based on immigration and invasion is "unusually liberating"; for whom is it true that "identity is portable; can be picked up, transported and constructed … on another shore"; for whom is it true that Australia's "unique" identity lies in "the good fortune of having undisputable borders"; and for whom is it true that "to abandon or allow [the institutions "we" brought here] to decay, would be an act of national suicide"?

For Malouf seems to speak rather too inclusively for modern Australia; to move from the warmly personal to the coolly national when he claims that "what we cannot remove is the language we speak, and all that is inherent in it", and that to abandon the institutions "we" brought here "would be an act of national suicide". As a teacher of a large cohort of children of post-war immigrants from many different countries, the questions I'm prompted to ask, not flippantly or merely rhetorically, is why should these Australians feel or care that their nation was "made in England"? What of the non-English-speaking or

English-as-a-second-language Australians who don't "recognise" the British "style" of their lives, language or institutions?

I believe there is an inheritance to be grappled with, and that these children in the end must care, but not for the same reasons as Malouf. For there is not just a British (or American) "style" to Australia's inheritance; nor should we reduce Britain's influence to a matter of aesthetics as so often occurs in "multicultural" Australia. As others have noted, the history of the British in Australia is "not just another multicultural story". To have been made in England is often – though not always – to have wielded power in Australia; the British are not just the "salt of the earth", as Pamela Bone argued in the *Age*. The power wielded (and yielded) has been significant (and aesthetics are political anyway).

And it is a power with which many Australians have had to grapple. We make ourselves "properly at home" and worry about "our own dispossession" as we attempt to appropriate identity and custodianship of the land from those for whom "invasion" is not an "unusually liberating" aspect of their identity. The power of our history of nationhood also challenges those who have left Australia's shores because our borders were heavily "disputable". Ultimately, I would argue, we must understand the British inheritance in Australia so we can negotiate aspects of its un-making.

I think this may also be a way in which Australia might develop more mature relationships with its "parent". Of course merely cutting the ties is impossible; certainly remembering the stories of migration – and the continuing state of migrancy – is a better basis for developing a sense of Australian history and identity. But this should apply also to the many features inherited from other countries whose migrants inhabit Australia today. Over a quarter of our population was born overseas. Over a third of our population has one or both parents born overseas. To paraphrase Malouf, these people do not see Australia "through eyes that have experienced the business of seeing only here, in the light as it falls in this place only; through what life has revealed to them, and would continue to reveal to them, only here".

Yet I welcome Malouf's essay – in some respects a risky argument in contemporary Australia for a writer of his stature. I also acknowledge Malouf's final disclaimer that "the conclusiveness of a full stop is no more ... than a pause in a continuing argument". But I welcome his intervention as an embodied response in a complex conversation, and not as shared national self-revelation. That I enjoyed much of the essay reveals much about my heritage and the tensions I bring to inhabiting Australia. Malouf states that: "Because we find it so difficult to imagine any history but the one we have actually experienced ... we tend to undervalue what was handed to us". Yes, but we shouldn't kid ourselves either that Englishness or Britishness in Australia has now "got away and become sexy". To be more sexy, Anglo-Australians will need to re-make the broad imaginary life of this country on the basis of acknowledging the inherited styles and languages of many others in this migrant nation.

Sara Wills

Gerard Windsor

David Malouf is that old-fashioned phenomenon, a cultivated man. He has the range of learning and interest that I would otherwise associate only with the great expats of his generation (Greer, Hughes, James, Porter). In spite of his fiction and poetry, opera is his idea of the supreme art, and he has written for it and about it. Galleries ask him to do introductions for exhibition catalogues. I have heard him sustain a discussion for over an hour on the more recondite archaeological sites in the Middle East with Mary Lovell, the biographer of the great Arabists Richard and Isabella Burton. Any reader of his fiction will know how deeply he has immersed himself in Australian history. With his Lebanese surname and ancestry, and his erstwhile apartment in Tuscany, we know that we have got a citizen of the world speaking to us.

His mother's people, however, were of English origin. In his twenties he too went to England and stayed and taught there for nearly ten years. But he came back. It would be heavy-handed to call him an Anglophile, but he's appreciative of England, and of what it's given Australia.

David Malouf has never been a polemicist; his style has always been too urbane for that. It is his way of being a native of this country. "Australia", he says, "is an experiment ... an experiment is open, all conclusions provisional. Even the conclusiveness of a full stop is no more, so long as there is breath, than a conventional gesture towards pause in a continuing argument."

These are the final words of *Made in England*. David Malouf's argument is less programmatic, less a pamphlet, than earlier essays. It's more discussion than argument, modestly asserting first the fact, and then the virtues, of England's progenitive relationship to Australia. Given its kindly attitude to England, the essay's most defiant feature is its publication in the week of the Rugby World Cup final – not an event the author shows any sign of adverting to. (Yet he does make the substantial point that organised competitive sport, such a mainstay and glue of Australian society, is a wholly Anglo-Saxon creation.)

This is a generous essay, determined above all to give credit – to Arthur Phillip, to the fitters-out of the First Fleet, the convict labourers, the anti-slavers, to a stable, enlightened Britain as a whole. It argues that the fall of Singapore did not turn Australians away from the motherland, that Britain's joining the European Union was a necessary turfing of the adult offspring out of the nest, that at least until recently, and with the exception of the movies, it was British not American culture that washed over us. There's room for debate on all such propositions, but the style of debate has been set – cheerful, moderate, reflective. More arguable, not least because it's such a big claim, is the contention that the threat of invasion in 1941 brought "Australia – the land itself – fully alive at last in our conscious-ness. As a part of the earth of which we were now the custodians. As soil to be defended and preserved because we were deeply connected to it. As the one place where we were properly at home …" This is affectionate towards the land, gen-erous towards fellow Australians, and instances a defining characteristic of this essay – its strong tendency to speak well of Australia and Australians. I'm not sure we quite deserve it. I have the uneasy feeling that although this passage is pur-portedly about 1941, it's actually a wish-list of sentiments for now. As a statement of fact about either 1941 or 2003 it's risky.

The overwhelmingly chewable ingredient, however, in this hamper of an essay is its point about language, the English language, the vital bond between England and Australia. D.M. defines an Anglo-Saxon habit of mind "whose most complete and perfect creation" is the English language. Language, he says, is what we come home to, and English has one huge distinction. Due above all to Shakespeare "the real motive force in English is metaphor … other languages move by logic … English, as we see from even the most common idioms – a 'tower of strength', 'a dog's breakfast' – by association." This is a gloriously bold claim to make, and for all the many virtues of *Made in England* I would like to read D.M. at the same length again on just this fingering of our native tongue. This is a linguist's debate, and I have no particular credentials as such, but all sorts of scraps and mementoes of other languages start prodding me into opposition against this claim for uniqueness. The phrase "tower of strength" for example brings to my mind the Latin of the Litany of Loreto (approved 1587) where the Virgin Mary is invoked under all manner of metaphorical titles that glori-ously ignite one another through their biblical associations – Mystical Rose, Tower of David, Tower of Ivory, House of Gold, Ark of the Covenant, Gate of Heaven, Morning Star … And if it's classical Latin we want, what could be more metaphorically aphoristic than Virgil's *Sunt lacrimae rerum* (there are the tears of things), or that great parable in five words, *Pariunt montes, nascitur ridiculus mus* (the mountains are in labour, a ridiculous mouse is born), or the three-word one, *Facilis descensus Averni* (the road to hell is easy).

The language of Shakespeare and his contemporaries was certainly suffused with metaphor, and this vivid colouring lasted for several generations. The linguotechnics of Sir Thomas Browne, for example, are a grand jumble of associations in pursuit of their tails. But Browne was dead a century before English was heard in Australia, and by the turn into the eighteenth century the frenzy of the language was calming down. The English who founded the colony at Sydney were the contemporaries of Gibbon. *The Decline and Fall of the Roman Empire* was written in the years between Cook's landfall in 1770 and Arthur Phillip's in 1788. John Gross's *Oxford Book of English Prose* has twelve passages from Gibbon, and the only metaphor that sticks its head up is a repeated variation on the notion of shades and clouds.

So where, linguistically, does this leave Australia? D.M. makes a point of the evolutionary nature of the English language, but having made his generalised point about its metaphorical core, he switches categories when he wants to point up the changes over 200 years. Metaphor is not mentioned again. Whereas a dominant but variable tone of the language is. The English of 1600 was "passionately evangelical and utopian, deeply imbued with the religious fanaticism and radical violence of the time". That's what America was given. Whereas the 1788 colony got an English that was "sober, unemphatic, good-humoured; a very sociable and moderate language, modern in a way that even we would recognise, and supremely rational and down to earth".

One of the enjoyable things about *Made in England* is that you want to argue with so much of it – and this summary of the English of 1788 sounds just too good to be true, a determinedly Whiggish reading of linguistic history. Roger Sharrock, in his introduction to the *Pelican Book of English Prose*, presents perhaps the other side of the coin. In the middle of the eighteenth century, he argues, "the language no longer remains a disciplined, neutral medium for the thought [but] the balance tips towards greater politeness and rhetorical control".

Ah, so Australians are children of an ultra-polite, to say nothing of a contained and gestural age? Maybe, maybe not, but D.M.'s thesis sounds just a little too nationalistically benign. English, he says, went through a period of reaction after the excesses of the English Civil War. It "had to be purged of all those forms of violent expression that had led men to violent action. By limiting one, you would limit the other. That was the program. The language itself was to be disarmed … And it worked." So that the revolution of 1688 was "bloodless" and the enlightened ameliorist progress in language and hence state of mind (or is it the other way around) continued throughout the next century.

This calculated engineering of history by … by whom? … is so stunning as to be implausible. In any case, the revolution of 1688 wasn't bloodless at all; it's just that the bloodletting was done across the Irish Sea. And the Monmouth rebellion of 1685, just three years prior to this new age of enlightenment, was put down with Judge Jeffreys's legendary savagery.

But what happened to the metaphor during all this? Far more noticeably than any violence of language, I would argue, metaphor is what has faded. Australian English has never been freely associational. Say too little rather than too much has been our motto. We shy away from the more decorative possibilities of the language.

Regrettably D.M. doesn't discuss the current state of this metaphorically based linguistic bond. What he does do is rather more conventional; he talks of the content rather than the form of the language. Anglophones "in their exchanges with one another can take it for granted that a great deal of what is being left unsaid, or exists in shades and nuances under what is said, as half-heard echoes out of plays, poems, novels, or out of the *obiter dicta* of occasions great and small in a shared history … will not go unrecognised, and may even be left to bear the burden of much that is subtly intended". The trouble is that D.M.'s examples of this *lingua franca* are the mots of Henry V ("once more unto the breach"), Sir Philip Sidney ("thy need is greater than mine"), Lord Nelson ("England expects …"), Howell Maurice Forgy ("praise the Lord and pass …"), all chestnuts of school storybooks of the 1940s and 1950s, but by now an almost completely withdrawn currency, at least in Australia. This unreality is repeated when D.M. says that "since the early decades of the nineteenth century most Australians … enjoyed the same reading [as their counterparts in Boston or Nottingham]: Walter Scott, Fenimore Cooper, Bulwer-Lytton, Dickens, Wilkie Collins …" D.M.'s own literateness seems to issue in wonderful optimism about the high cultural habits of "most Australians". I'm reminded of his calls for the reissue of no doubt fine works of Australian literature, but ones which remain resolutely out of print simply because only a risible fraction of Australians have any interest in buying and reading them.

On the strength of this essay there's no argument that Australia owes so many of its more admirable features to England. But the same language, the same state of mind now? What about starting with the two nations' preferred choice of spectator hymns? (Let's leave aside the imposed, longstanding official anthems.) The primary numbers on display during that great night at Homebush on 22

November 2003 were "Waltzing Matilda" and "Swing Low Sweet Chariot". They're a puzzle, both of them. Australians sing a bald narrative about a sheep thief, a ditty that obdurately refuses to be a metaphor for anything. The "waltzing matilda" of its title/chorus is, if anything, an anti-metaphor because it's ultimately inexplicable (cf *The Australian National Dictionary*), and it repudiates the essentially romantic nature of the device. The English spectators on that night cut through the obfuscating nonsense and reduced it to "I shagged Matilda." Or perhaps that was a metaphor, an utterly everyday and recognisable one, for the outcome of the match.

In any case, if it's language and state of mind we're talking about, what are we to make of a national hymn where at least five of the keywords – jumbuck, tucker bag, coolabah, billabong, trooper, and maybe waltzing for that matter – are fading, or have already faded, from public recognition? Can we really say the Australian state of mind is represented by words that are gibberish and describe an utterly alien experience?

And the English make no better sense. They cheer on their players by hailing the Grim Reaper's personal hearse. "Swing low, sweet chariot,/ Comin' for to carry me home,/ I looked over Jordan and what did I see?/ A band of Angels coming after me,/ Comin' for to carry me home." For a people at least as irreligious as Australians this is an astounding choice as a frenzy-enhancer. This language is far nearer to D.M.'s English of 1600 than it is to anything to be heard today in East Cheam or Grosvenor Square. It certainly doesn't display a state of mind that many Australians enjoy. I'm very confused. Pleasantly so. I want David Malouf to start again.

Gerard Windsor

First published in the *Australian Financial Review* on 5 December 2003.

| *Correspondence*

Patsy Millett

One must sympathise with Germaine Greer. Despite her solid grounding in academia and a reputation built on finely honed argument covering a wide range of subjects, she also serves another, lesser master. She is a seasoned television personality – indeed one might argue a child of the media known to the majority only via her appearances on the box – and she must be well aware of the exactions of its voracious maw. A scholarly dissertation on the theme of white Australians and the advantages of their accepting links with an inescapable Aboriginal heritage would not have raised much interest or propelled her through the available TV outlets – versatilely stern and forthright with Tony Jones on *Lateline*, mischievously flirtatious with Andrew Denton. The key to her long career as a hit-and-run artist upon our shores has been to ride in upon a white horse of indignation and/or outrage at some aspect of Australian failure – pronounce upon it loudly and prominently via the media – and depart. This time she has chosen a no less confronting line of attack in suggesting we are "guilty inheritors of a land that was innocently usurped by our ignorant, deluded, desperate forefathers". Her "big idea" is that the way out of our predicament is to admit we live in an Aboriginal country – go back to hunter-gatherer values and embrace our own Aboriginality. To support this whimsical proposition she cites many cases and examples of where our settlers failed and how as a result Australia as a nation is little more than a basket case. Taken at simplest level – which is all the popular media can cope with – Germaine Greer has blown in again this time telling us we should all become Aborigines. That certainly grabbed her the five minutes of attention she required to bravely (and articulately) air her views and remind us what a feisty old rabble-rouser she is.

The problem for me as a reader of *Whitefella Jump Up* was that while there could be little disagreement with her mixed bag of data from historical records and her overview of where we are going wrong, the whole did not credibly arrive at her remedial premise. Notwithstanding her straight-faced claim to being very serious indeed, it was of course a stunt. At best one should take with goodwill her plea that we sit on the ground and think. Unfortunately for the main line of the polemic, there was nothing unique about the mistakes made in the course of Australia's settlement by Europeans except that it was in comparison with every other colonisation in world history less violent and less destructive of land and indigenous cultures. (And ongoing alcohol abuse and environmental madness is hardly exclusive to our nation.)

Dr Greer herself must know the weaknesses in her argument and the refutations that are likely to appear in the correspondence section of QE. To ensure the spotlight for the short stretch of her visit she has however managed to put her topic confidently and boldly enough to at least temporarily camouflage the inconsistencies. She probably also knows that by selecting as a target for contempt that tall poppy of Australian literature *Kings in Grass Castles* with an incorporated attack on the author Dame Mary Durack there might be certain family sensitivities – such as that of this daughter – aroused.

In the introduction to *Whitefella Jump Up*, Peter Craven states that Greer is not preoccupied with the debates between Reynolds and Windschuttle – or the who did or did not do what to the Aborigines. Since the main source of contention in these so-called debates is the matter of accurate reporting, it is probably as well Greer avoids dipping her toe in these waters. (On what evidence for example does she describe Bedford Downs as "infamous"? Or is she merely repeating some vague hearsay as if it were historical fact?)

In citing *Kings in Grass Castles* as a prime instance of not only the ignorance of the pioneers but also the wrong-headed nature of their "land-grabbing" enterprise, Greer has allowed herself interpretations – and misinterpretations – of the book and the motives of the author that do nothing to bolster her case. In challenging some cavalier assertions made in the chapter "Going Native", I do not intend that Greer should get away with a dismissive "Well, they would object wouldn't they?" In writing the first of what she intended to be a trilogy, Mary Durack took the story from the point of view of the people involved. She avoided in *Kings* retrospective comment on the mores, motives and morals of the day. Although a certain amount of dramatic licence was introduced (it was never claimed to be an academic work) the book did not "purport" to be the history of the Durack family. Two decades of research went into the most accurate possible representation of a family chronicle. (What a mean little word "purport" is – implying that Mary Durack's version was unsoundly selective in its account.) In taking on such a broad sweep of history involving many characters and their complicated threads of connection, the author could not afford to dwell on any particular aspect.

She was of course guilty of writing history in such a way that it might appeal to the general public and of daring to hope that her labour of so many years might actually sell. She certainly did not envisage an acclaimed literary success that has from the time of its publication in 1959 never been out of print.

Mary Durack was not guilty – and here I take very strong exception indeed – of pretensions of grandeur. According to Greer the Duracks were descended from landless and illiterate peasants. Since Mary Durack makes this quite clear herself (though Patrick Durack and his siblings had rudimentary schooling and could read, write and figure) there is little point in scornfully underlining this fact along with the statement that the author has interpreted "flattering references" to a more distinguished "knightly" background "as if ... historical fact".

Professor Dermot Durack, a son of Patrick Durack resident in Ireland from 1922, spent many years before his death in 1956 researching the ancient books of Irish families, official and church records as far back as they went to follow the early threads of Durack history. A more careful reading will clearly show that while there is evidence of clan warfare, there is no claim to "knightly" honour and members of that branch of the family fondly holding to the French "Du Roc" connection were disabused of this fallacious belief. It is hard to see how the subject of (faithfully recorded) Durack genealogy adds any weight to Greer's argument. The inaccurate rendering gives the impression of being for no better purpose than to take a malicious and personal swipe at Mary Durack – whose modesty and lack of vanity were legendary.

One must also query Greer's denunciation of Mary Durack for her tendency to "romanticise the savage". Reproving of Mary Durack's vision (quoted in a passage that still reads with moving lyricism) of Aboriginal society as timeless and changeless until the coming of the white man, Greer then herself strays down utopia lane with an image of black Australians empowered with some sort of eternal key to conservation, land management and peaceful co-existence through the offices of their freely available spiritual consultancy. (Greer in Alice Springs claims to have experienced "a new kind of consciousness in which self was subordinate to awelye, the interrelationship of everything, skin, earth, language." Talk about DIY spirituality!)

Further critical and accusatory comments centre on Mary Durack's having written the wrong book altogether. Why, asks Greer in alluding to the close bond between Patrick Durack and the Aboriginal Pumpkin, was *Kings in Grass Castles* not the story of a lifelong friendship between a black man and a white man?

(Why, one could ask, did Greer when writing *The Obstacle Race* not concentrate on those women in history – from Toulouse-Lautrec's mother to Pollock's wife – without whose admirable support the work of famous artists might otherwise have been lost to us?)

The bond between two men who otherwise shared nothing in common is surely told with an economy of words that could scarcely be more affecting or explicit. Mary Durack has also sensitively depicted a mutual dependency which became the core of the ongoing black and white relations within the Durack pastoral company. To state that she saw the white man as indomitably superior supposes of the writer an insulting intellectual simplicity and a perception evident nowhere throughout her long writing career. Rather than expound upon this, may I suggest Greer read Durack's 1974 *Lament for a Drowned Country*.

To declare that "the ultimate purpose of a book like *Kings in Grass Castles* [name another "like"] is to elevate the squattocracy" is errant nonsense. One would be hard put for a start to include the Duracks, but for a brief period of prosperity, as "squattocracy" with its implied wealth and power. Their initial leaseholdings in west Queensland and later in the far north of WA certainly covered a vast area, but the era of tables decked with "damask and silver" scarce survived a single sitting. From the time of the 1889 financial crash the firm of Connor Doherty and Durack (CD&D) became a saga of unremitting toil in a largely profitless concern that from the 1920s fell into ever-mounting debt. To whatever extent Greer would point to this state of affairs as a result of their cited ignorance of the land and lack of proper regard for the wisdom of the Aborigines of the area, the fact is that the Duracks operated from primitive homesteads in singular discomfort. They paid for their incursion on virgin land with blood, sweat and tears. Mary Durack's intention was in fact to follow a pioneering family history – for better or worse – through three generations: the rags to riches and back to rags; the thrills and spills; the joys and heartbreaks; the interconnecting relationships both black and white ...

The ultimate fate of CD&D is signalled in *Sons in the Saddle*, the sequel to *Kings*. This book is largely constructed from the daily journal of M.P. Durack and the detailed documentation available. It is wrong to suppose that the family were – then and now – unaware or uncritical of the shortcomings of the one-hundred-year Durack pastoral tenure. The final volume (never completed) was intended as a more clear-eyed and personal view of the pioneering enterprise and its characters through Mary Durack's own involvement with the north and her long association with the Aboriginal people. She understood very well the conditions and failures of vision that thwarted and limited the chances of financial success.

The often troubled element of black and white relations was only one facet of a tangled whole. (It should be said in their defence, however, that the Duracks were a great deal more acceptable to the Aborigines than what replaced them.) Such clarity of vision does not accord with Greer's censure.

To allege that the author might have held a careless disregard for the importance of Aboriginal people is not only fallacious but wickedly so. Tellingly, Greer makes no mention of *Sons in the Saddle* and no hint of *The Rock and the Sand* – the latter a serious and sensitive social study of the confrontation between black and white with the arrival of missionary pioneers in the north-west.

Mary Durack's life might have been more profitably occupied had she not given so many years to the painstaking documentation of the mythology and genealogy of Kimberley and Dampierland Aborigines. Countless hours were spent with notebook and tape recorder in Aboriginal communities, and the memories – including of the Durack years – of these people have been preserved largely by her single-handed effort and her unstinting assistance to those who later continued this work.

In 1972 when Germaine Greer was making headlines with her condemnation of "disgusting conditions" for Aborigines in Alice Springs, Mary Durack was at the Adelaide Festival. To her alarm, she found herself confronted by the press – (unlike Greer, she never came to terms with thrusting microphones and pugilistic headlines) angling for a Lady of Letters versus Fuming Feminist "sound-bite". Anxious to present a more moderate viewpoint, Durack attempted to explain to her ADD inquisitors that the influx of Aborigines to northern towns was a downside of equal wage legislation and their consequential removal from their "born country" by station managers. Not that equal wages or in fact drinking rights could (as she further attempted to elucidate) in conscience be any longer withheld. Germaine Greer was right to note the depressing situation in Alice Springs, but – she continued – this was only one aspect of a brighter and more optimistic future for the preservation of Aboriginal culture and art forms through the Aboriginal Theatre Foundation convened in 1969 – to which organisation she had given much time as an Executive Member. But by now the press had got bored and melted away.

At the time Germaine Greer was giving us the benefit of her international perspective by being appalled, Mary Durack was one of the very few white people in Australia who could sit down on an equal level of affection and respect with a group of Aboriginal people and know their names, their history and genealogy. She did not speak of being "adopted by Aborigines" or such trite vanities. Seven years were given to the ATF (later the Aboriginal Cultural Foundation) on an entirely voluntary basis. The most consistent theme of her life's work involved Aboriginal themes – her deep feelings towards their situation past and present expressed in books, short stories, articles, talks and verse. To take her own chapter heading – "Who Does She Think She Is?" – who indeed does Germaine Greer think she is to presume to question Mary Durack's regard for Aboriginal people?

Putting aside more personal grievances, it is difficult to take seriously an academic who remonstrates against the first settlers' "mistakes" when such were listed in the lexicon of the day as enterprise, initiative, endurance, raw courage and, against all odds, a will to survive. Past damage can only be measured by taking into account universal white attitudes of the day – the awful God-fearing beliefs that so righteously colonised the world's far-flung reaches.

After a lifetime of close association and study, Mary Durack came to the conclusion that Australian Aborigines defied generalisations. Greer's essay relies upon them and in this failing alone "the shortest way to nationhood" falls apart. While Whitefella does need to Jump Up before we irrevocably lose our way as a nation, Greer's shallow handling of immensely complicated and multilayered subject matter just loses the plot.

Patsy Millett

John Benson

The issues discussed in Tim Flannery's Beautiful Lies raise a complex but important debate with major ramifications for how we manage the Australian landscape. The debate is about vegetation structure and fire ecology. It's also about the way simplistic statements made by reputable authors such as Tim Flannery can be used to justify ongoing damage to the Australian landscape.

First, I must refute some accusations Dr Flannery made in QE11 in response to a letter by the NSW Minister for the Environment, Bob Debus. Debus challenged Flannery's assertion that increased bushfire intensity is due to less regular burning and that a run of intense fires has caused species extinctions in places such as Royal National Park near Sydney. He argued that there are other explanations for species loss including the introduction of exotic predators and that the fires in the Park were due to extreme climatic conditions. Arson has also increased in recent decades. To support some of his case Debus cited a scientific review paper that I co-authored with Phil Redpath on the nature of pre-European vegetation and fire regimes in southern-eastern Australia.[1]

In his response to Debus, Flannery suggested that Redpath or I contributed to the Debus letter before it was published. This was not the case. Neither of us was aware of it until after it was published. However, we agree with its content. Although changed fire regimes may have played a role in some species extinctions in Australia, this has probably been insignificant compared to the impacts of domestic stock, exotic predators and European land use practices.

Flannery also asserted that we had published an "outright lie" about his writings on Aboriginal burning frequency. In our article we stated that the early explorers' statements were used to give an impression that burning took place annually. In his book The Future Eaters Flannery used the term "frequent" in describing Aboriginal burning practices. However, he failed to qualify this by mentioning Aborigines did not burn everywhere "frequently". The idea that Aborigines "more or less annually" burnt most of the country has been stated in

places such as the booklet prepared by Ryan et al, *The Australian landscape —
Observations of Explorers and Early Settlers*.[2] They refer to Flannery's writings to support
their case. This booklet is discussed below.

Fire and the mega-fauna

In *The Future Eaters*, Tim Flannery states that the Aborigines burnt the land "frequently". This supports his hypothesis of a human blitzkrieg that caused the
mega-fauna extinction. In brief, Flannery considers that the Aborigines hunted
the mega-fauna to extinction within 2000 years of their arrival 40,000–50,000
years ago. He proposes that this led to a profusion of vegetation that fuelled large-
scale bushfires which in turn led to the Aborigines frequently burning the bush
to control fuel levels. Flannery asserts that this frequent burning changed the previous vegetation into open grassy woodland and grasslands. He then asserts that
a cessation of Aboriginal burning since European settlement led to a regrowth of
shrubby vegetation and this caused species extinctions, particularly of medium to
small-sized native mammals. This is why in *Beautiful Lies* and elsewhere Flannery
suggests re-introducing frequent burning to manage the bush now.

To the lay reader this sounds like a plausible hypothesis – it is certainly inge-
nious in its scope. However, it is not supported by much scientific evidence and
it is likely that the hypothesis is wrong. Climate change over millions of years
was the main director of vegetation change in Australia. Fires have raged on this
continent for millions of years including during the times of the mega-fauna.
The evidence for this lies in soil cores and palaeo-botanical research, some of
which is beautifully summarised in Mary White's book *After the Greening: the
Browning of Gondwana*. Australia's flora have adjusted to the drying out of the continent as it drifted north into lower latitudes by developing hard wax-covered
leaves, reduced transpiration, hard woody seed coats, underground root systems
that allows vegetative re-sprouting and other features. Many of these features are
also advantageous to plants surviving fire.

Even if the Aborigines did rapidly extinguish the mega-fauna through hunting
pressure, other species would most likely have taken over their herbivore niches.
In any case, we know that invertebrate animals account for much of the herbivory
of Australian vegetation. As for the loss of small mammals due to cessation of
burning after European settlement, this seems an illogical argument since they
require vegetation cover to protect them from predators. Cover is lost with
frequent burning but is gained when there are long inter-fire periods. To add to
the debate, there is evidence that early graziers burnt some areas more than the
Aborigines (see our 1997 article for detailed references and discussion about

this). Furthermore, recent research at Cuddie Springs south of Walgett in north-western NSW by Judith Field of the University of Sydney points to an 8000-year co-existence (from 36,000 to 28,000 years ago) of Aborigines with the mega-fauna. If Field's data is accurate, it not only challenges Flannery's *Future Eaters* blitzkrieg hypothesis but also the consequences of that hypothesis about the scope of Aboriginal burning regimes. Field considers climate change may have played a major role in the extinction of the mega-fauna.

Regrowth and land clearing

The other aspect of this debate involves regrowth of vegetation and this relates to the discussion on fire above. The people who are the greatest advocates for clearing vegetation in NSW and Queensland are dry-land grain croppers, cotton growers and beef cattle graziers. Big agribusinesses are involved along with some wealthy farmers. Publications such as *The Australian Landscape – Observations of Explorers and Early Settlers*, professional rural lobby groups and influential individual farmers have used Flannery's and other popular writers' views about fire and regrowth to justify land clearing. They state that there has been massive regrowth of woody vegetation (shrubs and trees) due to a cessation of Aboriginal burning and by clearing it they are restoring it to a pre-European vegetation structure. This is largely nonsense but it has fooled some politicians and bureaucrats.

These people are clearing land to grow crops, not to restore some notion of a natural vegetation structure. If they were simply thinning regrowth it would be less of a problem for the environment. However, one cannot count a wheat crop as an environmental gain. Cropping wipes out most native species, destroys much of the soil biota and replaces them with an exotic monoculture. It's not as if we don't have lots of cleared country. In most parts of the Australian wheatbelt less than 20 per cent of the original extent of native vegetation remains. Yet they are trying to clear more of this despite documented species and ecosystem decline and the long-term ramifications of rising salinity levels to agricultural production. And they are pushing the grain belt further into marginal land at a time when climate change scenarios are predicting less reliable rainfall in these regions.

Nyngan is a town of about 3000 people on the western edge of the NSW wheatbelt. The surrounding countryside has moderate to poor soils and an un-reliable and relatively low rainfall. It is marginal cropping country. Some landholders want to convert grazing country to crops to cash in on the better commodity prices for grains than for sheep or cattle. This requires them to clear the country. In fact, they want to clear about 80 per cent of the private land in the region. Recently massive areas have been cleared in the region leading up to the introduction of new vegetation management laws in New South Wales. This has mostly been done without permission under current laws. The land clearers in the Nyngan region argue they are clearing "woody shrubby regrowth". However, in clearing the shrubs they sometimes also clear everything including old eucalyptus and wattle trees. More importantly, they are sowing annual crops so this radically impacts on the environment. The farmers say the woody regrowth is causing soil erosion and the shrubs have grown due to a lack of Aboriginal burning – thereby reflecting Flannery's writings. An expert science panel reviewed the literature on soil erosion in relation to woody regrowth. It reported that site management, seasonal conditions and grazing pressure are most important in determining ground cover and therefore erosion.[3] It is possible that the loss of topsoil after 150 years of excessive grazing, particularly during drought periods, may have created conditions that favour the survival of shrub species over herbaceous plants. Nevertheless, this does not suggest that shrub species did not occur in those areas, but rather are advantaged by the prevailing land management activities.

The creation of a myth

In 1995 a booklet was published titled The Australian Landscape – Observations of Explorers and Early Settlers. It was compiled by David Ryan, a former fire management officer with State Forests of NSW, Jim Ryan, an ex-hydro engineer and landholder from the town of Bredbo on the NSW Southern Tablelands, and Barry Starr who was then an employee in the former NSW Department of Land and Water Conservation (Murrumbidgee Region). The timing of the publication of this booklet coincided with the introduction of the first regulations in New South Wales to control land clearing. These regulations were in response to a public outcry over land clearing rates in New South Wales and the impact this was having on landscape functioning, river systems, wildlife and soil salinity.

The Ryan booklet was financed by the NSW Farmers Association and the former NSW Department of Land and Water Conservation. One could interpret it as a propaganda tool to convince those in power that clearing land was restoring the landscape to a notional natural state. It relied on the selective use of quotations from early explorers and some popular texts to support its case. One of these was Tim Flannery's The Future Eaters and Flannery has repeated similar statements in his essay Beautiful Lies.

In 1997 Phil Redpath and I exposed major flaws in the Ryan booklet. A review of its historical references showed that different interpretations could be made of journal passages when read in their full context and when other passages were taken into account. The scientific literature on species–fire interactions, also reviewed, cast further doubt on the claims in Ryan et al and in Flannery's writings on fire and vegetation. Yet the views of Ryan et al have been perpetrated as a myth by some farmer lobby groups, elements of the forest industry and others in order to justify frequent widespread burning and clearing native vegetation.

This is not just an esoteric academic debate. It impacts on the sustainable management of the natural resources of this fragile continent. It is about the way some loosely researched material in Tim Flannery's *The Future Eaters* and in his essay *Beautiful Lies* are taken as scientific fact and used by those intent on continuing the degradation of the Australian landscape for economic gain without being made accountable for the long-term effects of consequences such as salinity.

Other controversies

Much of *Beautiful Lies* is drawn from Flannery's earlier book *The Future Eaters*. I have no qualms with most of the essay's content including the sentiments expressed in the chapters titled "The Founding Lie", "White Liars", "The Colonial Drain", "Fighting for the Future", "Australia Adrift" and "Sweet and Sour Nation". These discuss some important social issues and matters to do with sustainable management of rural lands including the problems of over-allocation of water, soil erosion and degradation and salinity. Flannery is right to raise these big natural resource issues but he is wrong to criticise the benefits of the national reserve system and wilderness to the conservation of biodiversity and natural ecosystems and by default to our own sustainability.

Beautiful Lies contains several controversial statements, some of which were debated on the ABC Radio National *Earthbeat* program in April 2003. The participants in this debate were Flannery, a New Zealand whale expert Mike Donahoe, and me. Besides the issue of fire frequency, the debate covered these matters:

Cats: In his essay Flannery states that there is no evidence that cats caused the extinction of any species or animal in Australia. During the radio debate I handed Flannery a copy of a definitive review paper on this topic compiled by Sydney University researchers that reveals that up to seven species of animal may have become extinct due to predation by cats by 1850.[4] Other factors such as sheep and changed fire patterns may have played a role but you cannot state, as Flannery does in *Beautiful Lies*, that cats did not cause any extinctions.

Sustainable whaling: It seems Flannery fell for Japanese propaganda about sustainable harvesting of Minke whales by repeating their hypothesis that the relatively large numbers of Minke whales may be inhibiting the recovery of large, rarer whales such as the South Right Whale through competition for food. Mike

Donahue shot this hypothesis down by revealing that Minke whales eat different food than Southern Right whales and that illegal whaling by the Russians in the 1970s was mostly to blame for the lack of recovery of the Southern Right whale.

Wilderness, the reserve system and Aboriginal burning

In the chapter "The Dead Hand" Tim Flannery plays down the importance of the "flagship" battles won by the environment movement such as protecting special places such as Frazer Island and the Franklin River, stopping whaling, saving tracts of forest from the chainsaws and establishing a system of conservation reserves and wilderness areas to sample biodiversity and protect landscapes. He considers that reserves have failed to protect species from becoming extinct because they were intensely managed by Aborigines through the application of frequent fire and now are not.

Fire doubtless has a role to play in species management. By studying the ecology of a range of species that occur in an area, an appropriate fire regime can be implemented including through controlled burning if that is required. And burning to protect property is not in question here. However, species extinctions from natural remnants are most likely explained by the direct and indirect impacts of fragmentation of the landscape – a fact well established in scientific literature.

Taking Royal National Park near Sydney as an example, it is now surrounded by an urban sprawl, is encroached upon by domestic pets including dogs and cats, the voracious fox is common and pollution of waterways is difficult to control. These factors explain the loss of wildlife. You cannot just blame this on altered fire regimes due to a cessation of frequent Aboriginal burning. In any case we do not know how the area was burnt by Aboriginal people, although, paradoxically, recent charcoal evidence from Gibbon Lagoon near the town of Bundeena suggests that fire may have increased in frequency since European occupation of the region.[5] This is the opposite scenario to what Flannery suggests. Besides, when it comes to assessing fire frequency the most informative approach to study is the life cycle of a number of species of plants and animals that exist in an area.

Researchers have demonstrated that a fire-free interval in the order of 8–25 years is required to maintain biodiversity in shrubby sandstone country around Sydney, including Royal National Park. This possibly mirrors long term El Nino climate patterns. However, it needs to be emphasised that appropriate inter-fire intervals vary for different types of vegetation in different locations across Australia, a fact recognised in many bushfire management planning instruments.

In *Beautiful Lies* Flannery questions the concept of wilderness, suggesting it supports *terra nullius*. He has stated that the Aborigines managed all of the landscape therefore none of it (other than the uninhabited Lord Howe Island) was wilderness at the time of European settlement. In a recent article in the *Sydney Morning Herald's Good Weekend* magazine about the Wollemi National Park wilderness west of Sydney, Flannery was quoted as stating that Aboriginal people ought to be allowed to "hunt, use four-wheel drives and set up camps" because they originally managed these areas.

Over thousands of years Aboriginal people would have traversed every part of Australia but it is doubtful they intensively fire-stick managed all of it as was suggested in the 1950s and 1960s by anthropologists such as Tindale and Rhys Jones. Aboriginal numbers were limited (300,000–1,000,000 for the continent) and they concentrated mostly where Europeans now live or farm – on higher nutrient soils that produce more game and edible plant life. I agree that Aborigines may have regularly patch-burnt some grassy woodlands, grasslands, areas around camps and access routes. However, shrubby places such as Wollemi National Park are so low in nutrients it is doubtful that many Aborigines could have survived there other than for short visits, let alone intensively managed the whole 500,000 ha area. The recently discovered art sites in Wollemi may confirm the area was visited for certain purposes.

The biology of species reveals more about how places may have been burnt either by Aborigines or by natural fires. Many reserved lands in south-eastern Australia contain groups of plant species that are intolerant of being burnt every few years. Some vegetation types such as rainforest or saltbush cannot survive frequent fire at all and may become locally extinct. It is unlikely that Aboriginal people would have burnt too frequently if it affected food resources in rainforest or wetter forests. However, they may have regularly patch-burnt grassland areas to stimulate native yams that were a staple diet in south-eastern Australia. The point is that different types of vegetation were probably burnt differently by Aborigines. However, it beggars belief that such small numbers of people could have burnt the whole country all of the time as is suggested by some popular writers.

The national conservation reserve system and wilderness areas are the prime means of ensuring the survival of species simply because it is unlikely they will be grossly changed by humans. This contrasts with bushland on private land that is being cleared or over-grazed and some state forests that are being felled at unsustainable rates. At least our national parks are being professionally managed, albeit on limited budgets, by well-trained people who are dedicated to maintaining biodiversity. To downplay the importance of the national reserve system is foolhardy, yet this is what Flannery does in *Beautiful Lies*. However, most biologists (me included) agree with Flannery's call to improve the sustainable management of the ecosystems across rural landscapes as this is the matrix between the conservation reserves. This (mainly private) land is vital to the long-term survival of numerous species and to future agricultural production. For these reasons a number of scientific colleagues and myself have been calling for a cessation of broadscale land clearing for over a decade now and have endeavoured to persuade governments to help farmers rehabilitate over-cleared regions! In that decade about six million hectares of bushland in Queensland and between 500,000 ha and 1 million hectares of bushland in New South Wales have been cleared. The next year or so will see if the politicians are serious about stopping this onslaught. Most of the public certainly want it stopped.

After the ABC radio debate on *Beautiful Lies* Tim Flannery lent over to me in the studio and said "I guess I should do better checks on my facts." I agreed. Tim Flannery does himself a disservice by not doing so. He has a gift for writing and raises some important issues. However, he sometimes covers topics in which he lacks expertise and is therefore prone to make erroneous statements. These have been used by some as justification to destroy more land and wildlife habitat. Without losing his enthusiasm for environmental issues, Tim Flannery should check details more thoroughly when he pens articles for popular consumption.

John Benson

1. Benson, J.S. & Redpath, P.A., "The nature of pre-European native vegetation in south-eastern Australia: a critique of Ryan, D.G., Ryan, J.R. & Starr, B.J., *The Australian Landscape – Observations of Explorers and Early Settlers*", *Cunninghamia* 5(2), 1997, pp. 285–328.
2. Ryan, D.G., Ryan, J.R. & Starr, B.J., *The Australian Landscape – Observations of Explorers and Early Settlers*, Murrumbidgee Catchment Management Committee: Wagga Wagga, 1995.
3. Oliver, I., Eldridge, D. & Wilson, B., *Regrowth and soil erosion in central-west NSW. A report to the Native Vegetation Advisory Council*, Sydney, Department of Land and Water conservation, 2000.
4. Dickman, C.R., "Impact of exotic generalist predators on native fauna of Australia", *Wildlife Biology* 2(3), 1996, pp. 185–195.
5. Mooney, S.D., Radford, K.L. & Hancock, G., "Clues to the 'burning question': pre-European fire in the Sydney coastal region from sedimentary charcoal and palynology", *Ecological Management & Restoration* 2(3), 2000, pp. 203–212.

Acknowledgements: I thank Phil Redpath for commenting on the text. The views expressed are my own and are not necessarily those of the NSW government.

Tim Flannery

In his belated reply to my *Quarterly Essay* John Benson accuses me of a plethora of shortcomings, from conducting loose and careless research to perpetuating inaccuracies and aiding land-clearers. Such a spray is more in the nature of attempted character assassination than scientific debate, and cannot (nor indeed should it) be fully replied to here. Suffice to say that for a "loosely researched" book (which in fact took a decade of my life to research) *The Future Eaters* has stood well in academic circles: ten years after its publication it remains prescribed reading for many university courses both in Australia and the US.

A few of Benson's misquotations of my work do, however, need to be clarified.

1) Benson claims that I endorse the notion that Aborigines should be allowed to hunt in "wilderness" areas using four-wheel drives. A sensational headline, but utterly untrue. In fact what I said is that, in the spirit of Mabo, Aborigines with spiritual connection to sacred sites in national parks should be allowed to visit them, using four-wheel drives if necessary (an important concession given the fragile health of many Aboriginal elders).

2) Benson casts doubt on my hypothesis of mega-faunal extinction in Australia by citing "recent" research at Cuddie Springs. Yet he neglects to mention the most recent published research in this area, by Monash University archaeologist Bruno David and University of Wollongong geographer Richard Roberts, among others. Both have undertaken recent, detailed studies, with Roberts demonstrating that sand-grains of different ages are mixed together in critical layers at Cuddie Springs, and David showing that Aboriginal grindstones of a type that are less than 1000 years old elsewhere are mixed with the bones of mega-fauna tens of thousands of years old at the site. Such omissions make it hard to read Benson's comments as a serious attempt at engaging in the debate about mega-faunal extinction.

3) Benson says that I have given comfort to the land-clearers. What he fails to mention is that as a member of the Wentworth Group of concerned scientists

I was party to the largest reform ever made to land-clearing legislation in New South Wales, and have also been involved in the efforts to stop land clearing in Queensland (the fate of which currently hangs in the balance). The commitment of $460 million to stop land clearing in New South Wales is a direct result of the efforts of myself and my fellow Wentworthians. If land clearing is really the issue, why does Benson concentrate on the way my work was purportedly misused by others attempting to justify land clearing, yet entirely ignore the Wentworth Group's contribution to halting land clearing in New South Wales? Surely actions speak louder than supposedly misquoted words.

4) Benson says that in my *Quarterly Essay* I "play down" the efforts that led to the reservation of places like Frazer Island. I most emphatically do not do that. Instead what I do is point out the challenges ahead by acknowledging that significant extinctions have occurred, and continue to occur, in our reserved lands. Benson seems to think that I put these extinctions down solely to changed fire regimes. This is wrong. Clearly we need to manage all threatening processes.

The bottom line for me is that reserving the land is just the beginning (and that in no way denigrates those who did the reserving). The challenge facing us now is managing those reserved lands to maintain their full biodiversity – and this is something that we, as a nation, are patently failing at, for there is in all likelihood not a single national park in mainland temperate Australia that retains the full biodiversity it had in 1788. To adopt the "don't criticise" attitude of Benson in regard to reserved lands is, I believe, to fail those who worked so hard to reserve the lands and their biodiversity in the first place.

There are many critical issues in the areas I covered in my *Quarterly Essay* that will require long and tedious research to clarify. The role of cats in causing extinctions is one, mega-faunal extinction another, and the causes of the mysteriously delayed return of Southern Right whales to the Australian coast is a third. Many opinions exist on all of these matters, and as researchers in the general field we are entitled to debate all of them. But we are also obliged to contribute to the body of data that these debates are based on.

In my case I continue to do primary research into the timing and causes of mega-faunal extinction. In effect I'm constantly trying to falsify my own hypothesis, and I will be delighted if and when I or somebody else succeeds in this, for that is the way that science progresses.

The nature of burning in eastern Australia prior to 1788 is an area of national importance as well as an area of great professional interest to Benson. As one of Australia's few professional scientists working in fire ecology he has the opportunity to contribute primary research on this topic, yet I have seen very little by way of original contributions by Benson to this debate. Instead he wastes his time in attempts at denigrating my science and in misconstruing the things I say. It's about time that Benson and other like-minded individuals undertook the hard work of proving me wrong, rather than frittering away their time and mine with cheap shots and polemic.

Tim Flannery

Alan Atkinson is an ARC Professorial Fellow in History at the University of New England. His books include *The Commonwealth of Speech* (2002) and *The Europeans in Australia: A History*, Vols. 1 (1997) and 2 (forthcoming, August 2004).

John Benson is a Senior Plant Ecologist at the Botanic Gardens Trust, Sydney. He has published extensively on vegetation, environmental policy, threatened species and landscape management. He helped to establish the reserve system in New South Wales, was involved in formulating threatened species programs and more recently has been influential in bringing about natural resource reforms in New South Wales.

Larissa Behrendt is Professor of Law and Indigenous Studies and Director of the Jumbunna Indigenous House of Learning at the University of Technology, Sydney. Her latest book, *Achieving Social Justice*, is published by the Federation Press. *Home*, her first novel, will be published in May by UQP.

David Corlett has worked with refugees and asylum seekers both as a case-worker and a researcher. In 2003 he completed a doctoral thesis on Australia's response to asylum seekers. His writing has appeared in the *UNSW Law Journal*, *Dissent*, *Australian Quarterly* and the *Canberra Times*.

James Curran is the author of *The Power of Speech: Australian Prime Ministers Defining the National Image*, to be published by Melbourne University Publishing in April 2004. He is the John Curtin Prime Ministerial Library Visiting Scholar for 2004.

Tim Flannery has made contributions of international significance to the fields of palaeontology, mammalogy and conservation. His books include *The Future Eaters*, *Throwim Way Leg*, *A Gap in Nature* and *The Eternal Frontier*.

Morag Fraser is an adjunct professor in the School of Humanities and Social Sciences at La Trobe University. From 1991 until 2003 she was editor of *Eureka Street*.

Phillip Knightley's books include *Australia: A Biography of a Nation*, *A Hack's Progress* and *The First Casualty: A History of War, Correspondents and Propaganda*.

Robert Manne is Professor of Politics at La Trobe University and a regular commentator for the *Sydney Morning Herald* and the *Age*. His books include *In Denial*:

The Stolen Generations and the Right (2001), *The Petrov Affair* (new edition, 2004) and, as editor, *The Howard Years* (2004).

Patsy Millett is the daughter of Dame Mary Durack and her literary executor. She is currently working on aspects of family biography including the completion of the third volume in the Durack history begun with *Kings in Grass Castles*.

Sara Wills is a Lecturer and Postdoctoral Fellow at the Australian Centre, University of Melbourne, and a Research Associate with Museum Victoria.

Gerard Windsor is the author of eight books of stories, autobiography, essays and cultural commentary. His review essays appear in the *Australian Financial Review*.

QUARTERLY ESSAY

SUBSCRIPTIONS Receive a discount and never miss an issue. Mailed direct to your door. 1 year subscription (4 issues): $49.95 a year within Australia incl. GST (Institutional subs. $59.95). Outside Australia $79.95. All prices include postage and handling.

BACK ISSUES Please add $2.50 postage and handling to your order (or $8.00 for overseas orders).

- ☐ **Issue 1** ($9.95) Robert Manne's *In Denial: The Stolen Generations and the Right*
- ☐ **Issue 2** ($9.95) John Birmingham's *Appeasing Jakarta: Australia's Complicity in the East Timor Tragedy*
- ☐ **Issue 3** ($9.95) Guy Rundle's *The Opportunist: John Howard and the Triumph of Reaction*
- ☐ **Issue 4** ($9.95) Don Watson's *Rabbit Syndrome: Australia and America*
- ☐ **Issue 5** ($11.95) Mungo MacCallum's *Girt by Sea: Australia, the Refugees and the Politics of Fear*
- ☐ **Issue 6** ($11.95) John Button's *Beyond Belief: What Future for Labor?*
- ☐ **Issue 7** ($11.95) John Martinkus's *Paradise Betrayed: West Papua's Struggle for Independence*
- ☐ **Issue 8** ($11.95) Amanda Lohrey's *Groundswell: The Rise of the Greens*
- ☐ **Issue 9** ($11.95) Tim Flannery's *Beautiful Lies: Population and Environment in Australia*
- ☐ **Issue 10** ($12.95) Gideon Haigh's *Bad Company: The Cult of the CEO*
- ☐ **Issue 11** ($12.95) Germaine Greer's *Whitefella Jump Up: The Shortest Way to Nationhood*
- ☐ **Issue 12** ($12.95) David Malouf's *Made in England: Australia's British Inheritance*

PAYMENT DETAILS I enclose a cheque/money order made out to Schwartz Publishing Pty Ltd. Please debit my credit card (Mastercard, Visa Card or Bankcard accepted).

Card No. ☐☐☐☐ ☐☐☐☐ ☐☐☐☐ ☐☐☐☐

Expiry date   /   Amount $

Cardholder's name

Signature

Name

Address

Email

POST OR FAX TO:
Black Inc.
Level 5, 289 Flinders Lane, Melbourne,
Victoria 3000 Australia
Tel: 61 3 9654 2000 Fax: 61 3 9654 2290
Email: quarterlyessay@blackincbooks.com

Black Inc.

Subscribe online at www.quarterlyessay.com

www.ingramcontent.com/pod-product-compliance
Lightning Source LLC
Chambersburg PA
CBHW061247270326
41930CB00034B/3495